ADVENTURE GAMEWRITER'S HANDBOOK

By J. Walkowiak

A DATA BECKER BOOK

Published by:

You Can Count On Abacus Software

All commands, technical instructions, and programs contained in this book have been carefully worked on by the authors, i.e., written and run under careful supervision. However, mistakes in printing are not totally impossible; beyond that, ABACUS Software can neither guarantee nor be held legally responsible for the reader's not adhering to the text which follows, or for faulty instructions received. The authors will always appreciate receiving notice of subsequent mistakes.

First English Edition, March 1985
Printed in U.S.A.   Edited by Jim D'Haem and Russ Taber
Copyright (C) 1984 DATA BECKER GmbH
                   Merowingerstr. 30
                   4000 Dusseldorf, West Germany
Copyright (C) 1985 Abacus Software, Inc.
                   P.O. Box 7211
                   Grand Rapids, MI   49510

ISBN 0-916439-14-3

Table of Contents

1. INTRODUCTION

ADVENTURES are unusual human experiences characterized by extreme situations and dangers, indelibly impressed on the adventurer's memory.

They exert a great influence on the human mind and since time immemorial have fascinated even people not involved in the events. Poetry has made use of this fact, and in recent times various games of a literary nature have been developed.

First there were troubadors who told the people and crowned heads of the deeds of long dead heroes. Then in the 12th century the minstrels' poems developed into great epics such as "Lancelot".

"Don Quixote" inspired thousands with his experiences, following which travelers' tales [Defoe, Fenimore, Cooper etc.] made use of the subject of adventure, a development that stopped with the introduction of detective stories and sci-fi novels.

1.1 ADVENTURES TODAY

Who is not familiar with the adventure stories of their childhood or not been carried away by the experieces of <u>Lord of the Rings</u> or <u>Robinson Crusoe</u>? Who has not identified himself with the principal characters and imagined how he himself would have behaved in the same situation?

Most computer users, certainly in their early stages of computing, play space invader type programs. After a while though, when you realize that the playing sequence is always the same and that no thinking is required - just a quick wrist - boredom sets in.

However a recent survey reveals that the American computer users who enjoy arcade-type games have developed a strong following in ADVENTURE games. Lively adventures, along with chess or Othello, represent the most intelligent application of your computer for entertainment purposes. Now, in adventures, the field of play is not limited to you against a shower of aliens - but a whole world of situations and possibilities needing your understanding and logical thinking. Nimble fingers are not enough!

When an adventure program has been loaded into the computer, our computer contains an independent world, a world consisting of three-dimensional spaces, objects, and, last but not least, a large number of fellow players.

These fellow players must be able to communicate with us and must be able to hold a proper dialogue with us.

For example the principal character in an adventure is the figure with which we are to become ourselves. This principal character we best imagine to be a kind of robot that we control with words of our language. We instruct him to go in a certain direction. He then tells us what he sees at his new location. We instruct him to examine these things more closely, possibly order him to take them, and some time or other instruct him to use the objects in a certain way.

These programs allow us, without any great risk and at no great cost, to experience interesting adventure that may occur in the real world, but we can also enter a fantastic world full of ghosts and marvelous things; it is only the programmers' imagination that sets the limits.

A good adventure will cause us to act as in real life and will even let us explore space from the comfort of our favorite armchair.

Is it not far more interesting if, through the keyboard, I give an imaginary person the command "Open door" and the screen gives me the answer "I do not have the appropriate key" or "O.K. - the door is open" than if I continually press the firing button of my joystick to keep a counter and a tone generator running?

With the following examples I should like to show you how interesting it can really become:

How do we catch a fish in order not to starve when we have only our bare hands?

How can we keep the hungry bear from looking on us as a snack between meals?

How am I to cross the raging river inhabited by primeval predators?

With a little thought all these problems can be solved; we have only to have the right ideas and a lot of imagination.

Your task is to get into a certain house whose entrance is barred by an iron gate. By looking closely you see a key lying a few inches behind the gate, but unfortunately your arms are too short to let you reach the key through the gate.

How do you purpose getting into the house?

It is not possible to climb over the gate, but a few steps from the house you had noticed a number of trees. Some time or other during the game you also found a piece of chewing gum.

We spent some time solving this problem, mainly because no one had clearly pointed out objects that could have been used:

All we needed to do was to go to the tree and break off a branch. THen we returned to the entrance to house, chewed gum, fixed it to one end of the branch, pushed this end through the gate, and touched the key, whereupon this stuck to the chewing gum; by carefully pulling the branch back we finally got the key. And it fits the gate!

4

A neat solution, not so simple, but planned exactly in this way by the programmer during the development work. I should however add that the instructions enclosed with the game assume that the player has some experience in it.

Perhaps the above example has already put you in the mood for adventure. However, should you have not noticed the power of the written word to fascinate, imagine what it could be like if some really good detective novels were enacted on your computer.

Perhaps it will prove necessary one day to amplify the definition of the term "adventure" in our dictionaries as follows:

In the 20th century advanced computer technology made it possible for the adventure story also to play a part. Scott Adam's "Adventure Land" is regarded as a milestone; there followed many other adventures, developed to such a degree as to achieve "perfect world" simulations. Many well-known authors of books [for example Michael Crighton] promptly recognized the new possibilities and in their works created a balance for many people in relation to the everyday world.

1.2 THE HISTORY AND DEVELOPMENT OF ADVENTURES

Since a program-controlled computer brain was developed from the first computer, all kinds of efforts were made in programming circles to make computers simulate human thinking and human behavior. In 1966 Joseph Weizenbaum of the Massachusetts Institute of Technology developed his ELIZA program that finally succeed in interesting not only the experts, but also the public.

ELIZA, available today in slimmed-down versions for any microcomputer, simulates a psychiatrist and imitates the psychiatrist's typical way of talking. People used in the initial tests were very surprised to learn after their respective sessions that they had told a machine about their most personal problems.

Subsequent development of artificial intelligence resulted in the experts creating a program implemented on a PDP-10: **ADVENTURE - Colossal Cave**. For a change, the learned gentlemen were allowed to explore another field, that is look for treasure in a dark world governed by magic. **Collosal Cave** enjoyed great popularity among experts and was finally made available to fairly large numbers of the public in the summer of 1979. MICROSOFT, a firm probably known today to everyone, published **"Microsoft's Adventure"**, a diskette version of this original adventure for the most popular microcomputer in America then, the TRS-80.

The adventures were however made socially acceptable as early as 1978 by a young American names Scott Adams, who with his **ADVENTURE LAND** laid the foundation for the software firm ADVENTURE INTERNATIONAL.

This game, too, involves finding treasures in a mystical world, which naturally is made difficult by dragons, mazes, rivers of lava, and other dangers. Everything begins quite harmlessly in the middle of a woods. But when you have got your bearings and know in what direction you have to go to find the entrance to the underground kingdom, then ...

The demand for **ADVENTURE LAND** was immense, probably because at the time there were no other games of quality. Because of its great success, **ADVENTURE LAND** was quickly followed by a series of 12 adventures, skillful selection of the subject matter keeping the customer's interest alive.

Should you ever want to pick a fight with Count Dracula, you can in **"The Count"**. Or would you prefer to find a saboteur in an atomic power station? No problem, **"Mission Impossible"** makes it possible.

At this time there appeared on the American software market, a type of program called **"INTERACTIVE FICTION"**. These programs were supposed to represent a new type of literature and, as the name implies, were supposed to be books calling for participation. At first the player is only a reader. After the start of the program, he is very definitely brought into action. Numerous pages flicker over the screen. These give the reader information on what has happen before, the present situation, backgrounds, etc. and can be read just like a book.

Thus **"Local Call for Death"** begins just like a detective story. Three men meet in their clubhouse. During the course of the evening one of them is called to the telephone. It is the nephew asking his visibly excited uncle for money. The uncle refuses however to help him, knowing from experience that the money will be gambled away at the racetrack. The next morning he learns of his nephew's suicide.

At this point the player takes over. He represents one of the principal characters and endeavors to throw light on the apparent suicide by direct conversation with the participants.

A typical feature of these programs is the concentration on a single task, as in this case solving a murder.

To achieve this task, we as players must skillfully use questions more than objects. Which tends to be more interesting: "to read a conversation in a book?", "to follow a court case in a film?", or to "experience the success achieved in convicting a criminal?"

It is this very ability to hold dialogues that gives Interactive Fiction its appeal. A classic example is "Encounter in the Park", published by Adventure International.

In this game we meet our dream woman during a morning walk and it becomes our intention to enchant this girl and persuade her to consent to marriage. The programmer has given the player a wide spectrum of persuasive arguments, and it really is a lot of fun to find out how the lady reacts to certain suggestions.

The worst that can happen to us if we make suggestions that are too frivolous is that the lady turns away from us incensed and we spend the rest of our life in monastery.

As already said, all these textual adventures proved to be of very great interest and accordingly a growing number of firms published more or less good copies of these games. With increasing pressure from competitors a number of software manufacturers started thinking about new generations of adventure.

There appeared the first **MAZE ADVENTURES**, the aim of the game being to escape from a building, but nearly always the player got hopelessly lost in the maze, shown in perspective on the screen. The next stage of development was the **QUEST ADVENTURES**, which in most cases were implemented as real-time adventures. Here the player is subjected to additional stress, for unless on the appearance of some robbers he does not immediately input F for Fight and then does not continually press certain keys or combinations of keys in order to brandish his sword, the game ends very early because the main character is too badly injured to continue.

Unfortunately the conception of these games greatly restricts the player's freedom of action, since he is left with only a few actions such as fight, negotiate, buy, or flee on the menu.

The next stage in the development of adventure games was made possible thanks to the falling prices for graphic processors and RAM modules, for now it was no longer difficult for computer manufacturers to offer home users inexpensive computers with graphics, previously available only on much larger and therefore much more costly equipment.

With the sale of the first **GRAPHIC ADVENTURE** these games were given a new boost in 1982 [somewhat earlier in the case of Apple users], for while they had been frowned upon by many computer users as pure textual games, they now suddenly became interesting because of the many colorful pictures; in addition they proved eminently suitable in their ability to elicit at least an astonished "Oh, that's nice!" from relatives not familiar with computers, following the question "What can your computer do then?".

Naturally nothing at all had changed in respect to the value and aim of the game. Suddenly further groups came within reach: a reason for flooding the market with many well-known adventures in the new garb, adventures that had been known for years; the detailed descriptions had disappeared and instead the current situation was to be seen on the television screen.

Whether as a result the programs had become better or easier to play is an open question. I personally prefer to have my attention drawn to important things by a statement such as "I am in the woods. There are nothing but trees around me. Between two oaks I see a hole in the ground." than, in contrast, to see only a few trees; I then regard these as appearing a bit too early for an otherwise quite normal part of woods, for which reason I move on quickly, examine the trees no further, and as a result naturally overlook the hole, a small patch on the monitor. Needless to say, a successful conclusion to the game is not possible.

2. THE CONCEPT

2.1 PREPARING THE ADVENTURES

In the following chapters of this book we shall develop a
number of adventure games together. Of course we want to
give our work as professional a look as possible, so we
shall not be able to avoid analyzing the properties and
special features of programs already on the market.

Then we shall think about how we can program the individual
functions in BASIC.

It has already been emphasized that an adventure is intended
to move the player to another world, a world that makes the
impossible possible. He is intended to experience
adventures here, so he must be able to move and act.
Likewise the results of his efforts must be communicated to
him. Sensible, planned action is not however possible for a
human being until he has used his senses. The information
that in real life the adventurer picks up with his eyes,
ears and sense of touch must therefore be offered to the
player in another manner.

Since the human brain cannot as yet be connected direct to a
computer, we obtain answers to the questions "Where am I?",
"What do I see?", "Where can I go?", "What do I feel?", and
"What do I see?" in the form of short, but complete
sentences.

11

A conscious understanding of the environment will of course not be possible except in the rarest of cases. Therefore the adventure player cannot be expected to study extensive treatises on the world he has just entered, otherwise he will never identify himself with the character in the game and indulge in the illusion of a fictitious world.

Therefore, unless it is a question of graphic games, the monitor picture is divided into two clear zones, each of which has a precisely defined function.

The upper half of the picture will tell us where we happen to be and what we see, while the lower half is intended for communication with the main character acting for us in the adventure. Here we input our instructions and learn what happens following our inputs.

In this way we are enabled to move on in an imaginary world in accordance with a set plan, just as we are enabled to carry out sensible manipulations and actions.

A typical screen picture could look something like this:

    I am in a dark wood.

    I see a lot of old trees.

    I can move north, east, west.

    What am I to do?

12

Should we intend to advance as quickly as possible in the game, it would be wrong to walk aimlessly in the direction of one of the three cardinal points. The most obvious thing for an adventure player to do in any situation is to examine everything as carefully as possible. Thus possible answer to "Examine tree" would be something like this: "They are old oak trees" or "Here the trees are dying off all around".

These answers, it is true, do not help us, but apparently only show us that after all it is not always important to examine everything. But how is one supposed to know the answer in advance? For even an answer like "In the tree trunk I see an opening" would have been possible. Perhaps it is an old nest made by a woodpecker with part of the treasure concealed in it; "Examine opening" will throw light on the matter.

If we did not find any clues, even following "Explore wood" [it could be magic wood], we should have to decide where it would now be sensible for us to go.

How would you behave in such a situation, without map and compass, helpless and alone, far from all paths? Presumably you would climb up a tree in order to see what there is in the immediate vicinity and in the distance.

Therefore your input should read "Climb tree" and if you do not receive a statement such as "I am not athletic enough for that!", the picture on the monitor will change:

I am in the crown of an old oak tree.

In the north I see a mountain range,

in the east a lake,

in the west rising smoke.

I can go down

CLIMB TREE

Okay!

What am I to do?

The situation now looks a lot better, since following the
input of D for Down the only problem we still have is to
decide which area we want to visit first.

The statement "Okay!" tells us that the input has been
understood and executed. Had that not been so, we should
have received "I do not understand the verb" and the program
would undoubtedly have caused us to use a different mode of
expression. The same applies to to the object of our input.

Conceivably there are two other answers. In one case we
shall often receive the statement "I must be stupid,
but....- I do not understand what you mean!" With this the
program intends to tell us that the words used do belong to
the programmed vocabulary, but that at the moment the
command is not a sensible one: "Take key" will be

understood by the adventure program if a key appears in the
adventure, but becomes meaningless if the key is not in the
same space as the player.

The position is similar with the second standard statement
"You can't do that ...yet." Should we get this answer, we
may breathe a sigh of relief, for we are on the right way;
the only thing is that not all the necessary conditions for
execution of the command have been fulfilled. Thus a locked
door cannot be opened unless we have the appropriate key.

2.2 STANDARD FUNCTIONS OF THE ADVENTURES

In an average adventure we find 30 - 35 different three-dimensional spaces and in each space one or more objects. These objects in turn can contain other things, and as one never knows exactly what will be needed in the adventure, they take with them everything that gets into their hands and is not too heavy to carry.

It becomes very difficult to maintain a perspective, since we naturally do not make notes.

Fortunately programmers quickly recognized the situation, with the result that today after input of INVENTORY every adventure prints out on the screen all the objects that we carry with us.

Should the adventure be a friendly one or one written specially for beginners, it is possible for us in some situations to obtain tips, since then the command HELP may be implemented.

As distinct from the standard input consisting of verb and object, what is involved here, as in the case of Inventory, is a one-word command that will initiate an action, but can do many things:

"I would examine everything" shows our negligence. On the other hand the statement "A fairylike figure appears and writes the sentence "Open sesame" in the sand will in a confusing situation cause us to jump for joy.

Things look worse if we have to pay for the help:

A troll appears and says that we are having 10 points deducted for his help. He wants to know whether we need help.

Presumably in such cases dark clouds will appear on the horizon. If on inputting "help" we get the message "Help is not provided for in this adventure!" or if in answer only the general playing instructions are repeated the we know help is not provided.

No doubt it may be annoying if, despite all your efforts, you cannot move on when a certain point is reached, but no one should regard the last two examples as an act of malice on the part of the programmer. If the help function were guaranteed, some particularly clever people would solve the adventure in 30 minutes, but would never appreciate the fascination of such a program.

2.3 THE FIRST STEPS TO YOUR ADVENTURE

The general structure of the adventure games is now known to us. We have some idea of how our adventure has to present itself on the monitor and what functions we have to implement as standard.   In what follows we shall therefore think about the individual elements of our adventure system and about achieving them through our programming.

2.3.1 SPACES in the adventure:

The adventure world is composed of the spaces in the particular game concerned, that is to say each place that can be reached by the player wandering about in the adventure is called a space.   It's size is   totally irrelevant. As in our previous examples, it can be woods or the crown of a tree or the inside of a car or a mine.

The individual spaces so far as the player is concerned are distinguished by their descriptions and their geographical arrangement;   from the programming point of view, as we shall see, they are distinguished by their space number.

All these spaces can be reached by the player and must therefore be joined together in some way or other. In every adventure it is possible to move in the direction of all four cardinal points [north, south, east and west].   Some allow movement also in a vertical plane.   Needless to say, however, a situation in which the player leaves space 5 in a westerly direction, enters space 6 from the east, and wanting to return to space 5, cannot find a way in an easterly direction, or, worse still, gets into space 5 again

by moving down must not be allowed to arise. Here again the
exception proves the rule, for what would an adventure be
without a magic maze?

2.3.2 OBJECTS

Most "spaces" have "objects" contained inside them. We must
accommodate all objects in the spaces or, more correctly
expressed, allocate a space to each object. With this
allocation we automatically ensure that no objects are
duplicated.

A further problem that presents itself is the placement of
objects that must not be in the adventure at the beginning
of the game. Where do they stay until they appear?

Let us assume that our hero enters a space and that only an
old, locked wooden box is discovered, it being the only
visible object.

Following the player's input "Open box" all the rules of the
logic demand that the old, opened box should appear, filled
possibly with silver coins.

The solution to these problems will not present us with any
particular difficulty. In our adventure we shall install an
additional space, the STOREROOM, and in it store all objects
not presently being used. If we do not program any
connections to this space, the player can never enter it.

2.3.3 INPUTS

In this chapter we shall see how simple it is to program the storeroom and the entire adventure world; later on in the book we shall see the need for further SPECIAL SPACES.

As already seen from the preceding text, the player's inputs consist mostly of a verb and an object. Our program must therefore first test whether the input is allowed, for which purpose separation into verb and object becomes essential. Should the player have written something incorrectly or should the verb used not be provided for, a suitable message must be given. If our adventure finds the input verb in its vocabulary again, the object must be checked in the same way.

If both words are defined, the program can react in the manner prescribed.

When compiling this vocabulary, the programmer must exercise particular care and anticipate all possible inputs that a player could make. If the player takes too long in making his wishes clear to the adventure, he will quickly lose interest.

2.3.4 MESSAGES

Naturally the execution of a command must be made clear to the player. In the simplest case this is done with "O.K.", but usually additional messages are output. The most varied inputs often require the same answer, so the sensible thing to do is to make a table with specific standard messages.

2.4 THE IDEA OF THE GAME

With this we have mastered the minimum of dull theory. Now
we can switch on our Commodore 64 and begin some practical
work.   Perhaps you already have some fixed idea of your
first adventure. If not, allow yourself to be inspired by
the following suggestions.

1. THE HAUNTED HOUSE

You receive a letter from your aunt, her last
letter in which she bequeaths her old, palatial
home to you.   There is however a note that is
supscious, a note to the effect that you should be
careful, otherwise what happened to your uncle
could happen to you.   Such talk does not stop you
visiting the house. Immediately you find all sorts
of inconsistencies, you find a secret library with
books on necromancy, and in the cellar discover a
sacrificial alter.   Innumerable ghosts make life
difficult for you until you finally discover that
one of your ancestors murdered the sect leader in
order to increase his own power and by way of
punishment was buried alive.   You are now to help
him to find eternal rest.

2. THE OLD MAN'S LEGACY

Your friend and neighbor, a famous scientist, has
died in mysterious circumstances.   You receive a
note in which he asks you to complete his life's
work.   When you have managed to get into his

21

secret laboratory, it is your job to put his supercomputer into operation. The computer then gives you further information.

3. STAR ODYSSEY

Your spaceship is so badly damaged by a cosmic storm that you have to land on an unmanned station in order to get replacement parts to enable you to return to Earth.

4. GOLD FEVER

In the wilderness you meet a mortally wounded old man, who tells you about his goldmine. He shows you a number of pieces of gold and tells you that he has hidden more gold at several different places in the mine and that because he no longer needs it you may take it for yourself.

I should like to take the latter suggestion, an adventure involving a treasure hunt, as a basis for the next chapters in this book and elaborate upon it with you. Needless to say, you are free to realize any idea of your own, but in the case of all examples still to be introduced I shall repeatedly make reference to Gold Fever.

3. PROGRAMMING YOUR ADVENTURE

3.1 FORMING THE WORLD

With the selection of the subject the rough course of events
in the adventure is already established. In what follows we
shall work out a number of structures and go on improving
them until a world planned down to the last detail has been
created.

We shall do exactly the same with the programming; we shall
build up our adventure step by step and repeatedly satisfy
ourselves that the individual routines are functioning
correctly.

However, in order to be able, if necessary, to exchange or
supplement individual parts of the program, I should like to
ask you at this point to use only the specified line
numbers.

3.1.1 THE MAP

At the beginning there is nothing.   In what follows however
we shall use our imagination to create the world so urgently
needed for our game.   What our world has to offer is
determined by the subject.   **Gold Fever** will presumably take
place in and around a mine.

Let us just imagine the mine: a fissured, boulder covered
slope; a tool shed; wooden troughs bringing water from a
mountain stream for washing the gold; rotten, dry wooden

beams lining the dark entrance; dark passages full of
danger.

No doubt many similar pictures will easily occur to us and
make us find a sufficient number of spaces for the action
planned.

I should first like to limit our example to just six spaces.
Let us begin with a walk through a wood to the mine, where
our task will be to look for the treasure.

We can content ourselves with finding all the treasure, but
we can also set the adventurer to the task of depositing the
treasure in a safe place. For the time being, however, let
finding the gold be enough.

The task and objective has been fixed, also two essential
places, one the woods, which we shall build up out of two
spaces, and the other the mine. It is of course clear to us
that we cannot develop any action in this small world, for
we need room in order to be able to hide a number of objects
and set a few traps for the player.

Normally a mine will not begin between the roots of a tree;
we must create suitable crossings in the landscape to make a
realistic game possible.

Three further spaces provide us with sufficient room for
working out the first version of our adventure, and we can
now draw up a list of all the places involved.

in the woods

the edge of the woods, bound by a sloping rock face

a clearing in the woods

a clearing in the woods on the mountain slope

the entrance to the mine

To complete the program, the next step is to produce a map in which all the places are represented by rectangles. These are numbered consecutively and given their space description. Here we pay attention to the phrasing to allow for the line length of 40 characters of our Commodore 64. Our description must follow smoothly from the introductory text "I am". What number the individual space gets is of no importance. We have only to begin with one and go on counting consecutively, thus avoiding duplicate numbering. Following this we join the spaces together and at each boundary note down the corresponding cardinal point.

It can now readily be seen from this map that if for example the player is in space 3, the following messages have to be output on the monitor.

"I am in the woods. In front of me there is a steep sloping rock face".

In addition our map gives us information on the possible directions of movement:

"I can move west, south."

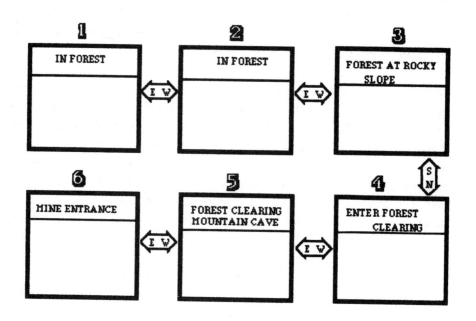

For each space in our program we could now program a
condition such as ; if the player is in space 3, then print
"I am in the woods. In front of me there is a steep sloping
rock face.", but then we should have soon filled the memory.

The principle is however correct.   We shall store the space
descriptions in a field of variables, to which we sensibly
give the name SPACE.

3.2 Variables and Fields

In order to store intermediate results or data relating to a program, variables are used in every computer language.

These variables act like small pigeon holes in which something can be deposited for safekeeping. These pigeon holes have names [file cabinet or desk drawer would be possible]. Then there are pigeon holes of the same kind: drawers 1,2,3, etc. in a desk, one below the other. Each pigeon hole is called a drawer and differs from the next only in its number. It is the same in Basic. We can give each variable a name of its own and an index number. This is then written in brackets behind the name of the variable.

Here two fundamental types of variables can be distinquished. One takes only numbers, numbers that can be used for calculation, while the other is used for texts. The composition and length of the texts are not important, or, more precisely, we want to allow every character on our keyboard and lengths of up to 255 characters one after the other.

A few examples of correct variables would be: A, A1, A2, TE1 [only numbers], TEXT$1 [for texts] as simple variables, A[1], A[2], A[3] as subscripted variables.

Perhaps you have already seen someone trying to brighten up their homes with letter cases filled with small miniatures [such cases were created for keeping the small letters used by printers]; let us beginners now visualize each individual letter case as a variable.

To have a practical example immediately to hand, let us do
the following, preferably only in thought:

From our adventure map we cut out the rectangles of the
individual spaces. We place each of the rectangles in a
separate case, taking care however to ensure that the
earlier arrangement of the spaces is retained, that is to
say our woods lies right at the top on the left, while the
entrance tunnel is located in the second row on the left.

To the question "Where is the mine?" we could answer "In the
first column of the second row." Likewise the positions of
all other spaces are determined by the row and column co-
ordinates. In computer languages this arrangement is called
a two-dimensional array.

In BASIC we would call our letter case the variable field
MAP$ [$ because texts are to be stored] and allocate the
following contents to the individual variables:

MAP$ [1,1] = "in the wood", first row, first column
MAP$ [1,3] = "clearing in the wood", first row, third column
MAP$ [2,2] = "entrance to the mine" etc

Therefore we input the following program text:
```
    500 REM----------SPACE DESCRIPTIONS
    501 SPACE$ [1] = "in the wood"
    502 SPACE$ [2] = "in the wood"
    503  SPACE$ [3] = "in the wood in front of a  rocky
    slope"
    504 SPACE$ [4] = "in a clearing"
    505  SPACE$ [5] = "in a clearing at the foot  of  a
    mountain slope"
```

```
506 SPACE$ [6] = "at the entrance tunnel to an old
mine"
```

This establishes the spaces in our computer. The only thing
missing is the character that moves in the programmed world
and describes to us the situation in which it happens to be
at any given moment. Its location will naturally be
dependent on our inputs; therefore we introduce a further
variable, which we will call PLAYER. This variable stores
the player's position at any given time.

Meaningful values for this variable are the figures one to
six, since PRINT SPACE$ [PLAYER] then prints out the
respective descriptions of the location "space". For test
purposes let us input the next lines:

Note: I should like to ask you once again to retain the line
numbers specified, as some of the lines are changed with the
subsequent development and unused numbers are occupied by
additional program lines!

```
1140 PRINT"I am"
1150 PRINT SPACE$ [PLAYER]
1390 INPUT "MOVE PLAYER INTO WHAT SPACE"; PLAYER
5000 GOTO 1140
```

This makes reconnaissance in our world possible, but the
method of progression is in no way satisfactory. We do not
want to jump at random from one space into another, but
strive to take specific bearings from the cardinal points.

Normally the space just visited by the player will have at least one or a maximum of six exits. In the east space-2 joins space-1. No exits lead in the directions north, south, and west or up and down. If we agree that the cardinal points are always named in the sequence N, S, W, E, UP and DOWN, space-1 can be specified as follows:

        1 in the woods   -, -, -, X, -, -

Appropiately exits are not then marked by an x, but the space to be reached in this direction is explicitly indicated:

        1 in the woods   0, 0, 0, 2, 0, 0
        2 in the woods   0, 0, 1, 3, 0, 0

These six values are stored in a variable for each space [let us call it PASSAGE]. Since here two different values [space and direction] indicate the space to be entered, storage in a two-dimensional array is appropriate, the row in each case being equal to the space and the columns, one to six, corresponding to the possible ways.

SPACE	N	S	W	E	UP	D
1	0	0	0	2	0	0
2	0	0	1	3	0	0
3	0	4	2	0	0	0
4	3	0	5	0	0	0
5	0	0	6	4	0	0
6	0	0	0	5	0	0

It should not be difficult for anyone to program this direction table [also called a travel table].

Beginners who do not understand the next lines are asked to
refer back to our previous example based on a printer's
letter case.

```
101  PASSAGE [1,1]=0 : PASSAGE [1,2]=0
102  PASSAGE [1,3]=0 : PASSAGE [1,4]=2
103  PASSAGE [1,5]=0 : PASSAGE [1,6]=0
```

The above lines program the passage from space-1 to space-2
in an easterly direction. We could proceed likewise with
the other spaces, but that would be very wasteful as memory
is concerned [how often do we write "passage"?].   Moreover
the immense amount of typing is not a particularly enjoyable
job.

For this reason we dispense with lines 101 to 103 and at
this point prefer to use the commands DATA and READ. Please
delete line 101-103 from your computer's memory.

3.3 READ & DATA

Generally we use the INPUT instruction to pass data to a
running program via the keyboard. It has the form INPUT VAR
[VAR can be any desired variable]. For sequential inputting
of several variables, DATA statements are used.   Data
separated by commas, is added to our program: INPUT LENGTH,
WIDTH, HEIGHT can accordingly be three figures in the
program listed one after the other, which are then
available for further processing.

If the data is known at the start of the program, they can
be incorporated directly into the program, which naturally
makes sense only if they are always the same for each
program run.   The keywords necessary for this purpose are
READ and DATA. INPUT is replaced by READ: READ LENGTH,
WIDTH, HEIGHT therefore performs the same function, and the
input data is stored with DATA 1, 2, 3 in any desired
program line.

It is important to know that the data is read in sequence.
Therefore the number of data in DATA lines must be equal to
the number of variables in READ instructions, otherwise
there will be an error message or not all the data will be
read.

If the data is to be read in again, beginning with the first
element, the command RESTORE must be used.

Therefore we input the following lines into our 64:

```
500   REM -------------SPACE DESCRIPTIONS
501   DATA "IN THE WOOD"
502   DATA "IN THE WOOD"
503   DATA "IN THE WOOD IN FRONT OF A ROCKY SLOPE"
504   DATA "IN A CLEARING IN THE WOOD"
505   DATA "IN A CLEARING AT THE FOOT OF A  MOUNTAIN
SLOPE"
506   DATA "BY THE ENTRANCE TUNNEL TO AN OLD MINE"
```

The data must now be transferred to the work variables.
This allocation is done by READ SPACE$ [I].   [I] takes the
space numbers one to six in sequence.   To avoid errors, the
number of spaces must be known; we introduce the variable NS
- number of spaces. They should be initialized right at the
beginning of the program text.

```
110   NS=6
```

Using a loop the space descriptions are read in:

```
845   FOR SPACE=1 TO NS
850   READ SPACES [SPACE]
870   NEXT PAGE
```

In the same manner our direction table is implemented; to
keep an overall view, we write the direction values into
respective data lines directly behind the space
descriptions:

```
500   REM ----------- SPACE DESCRIPTIONS
501   DATA "IN THE WOOD", 0,0,0,2,0,0,
502   DATA "IN THE WOOD", 0,0,1,3,0,0,
503   DATA "IN THE WOOD IN FRONT OF A ROCKY SLOPE",
```

```
          0,4,2,0,0,0
    504   DATA "IN A CLEARING IN THE WOOD", 3,0,5,0,0,0
    505   DATA "IN A CLEARING AT THE FOOT OF A MOUNTAIN SLOPE",
          0,0,6,4,0,0
    506   DATA "AT THE ENTRANCE TUNNEL TO AN OLD MINE",
          0,0,0,5,0,0
```

The possible exits must be read in together with the
descriptions. Since six direction data items follow each
space, a second loop is constructed within the first:

```
    855   FOR DIR=1 TO 6
    860   READ PASSAGE [SPACE,DIR]
    865   NEXT DIR
```

Accordingly each row of our array is identical with a space;
in the six columns of each row are stored the space that the
player can enter by inputting the direction concerned.

With this arrangement it will be possible for us using a very
simple method to achieve the player's progression.

However, before the player can turn in any direction at all,
he must be able to find out which ways are available to him.
Therefore we must develop a number of program lines that
print out the free cardinal points on the screen.

Let us assume that our principal character is at present in
space 3.

Row 3 of our direction table is now consulted:

SPACE	N	S	W	E	UP	D
1	0	0	0	2	0	0
2	0	0	1	3	0	0
3	0	4	2	0	0	0
4	3	0	5	0	0	0
5	0	0	6	4	0	0
6	0	0	0	5	0	0

All we have to do is output the designations of those columns that contain no zeros; in our special example columns two and three, south and west.

As we have established, the row in the field is identical with the space to be examined; to keep this actual space number ready, we have previously introduced the variable PLAYER. Therefore, to output the unblocked directions, our program must test the six directions of the space SP and print out the names of all columns that are not equal to zero.

Six directions must be checked:

```
1250 FOR DIR=1 TO 6
1260  IF PASSAGE (PLA, DIR)<>0, THEN PRINT
"** EXIT **"
1310 NEXT DIR
```

In a test run our program will now describe each space and indicate each possible exit, but unfortunately not its direction. Therefore we prepare a further field, a field with the designations of the direction [DIR$]:

```
1020 DATA NORTH, SOUTH, WEST, EAST, UP, DOWN
1030 FOR DIR=1 TO 6
1040 READ DIR$ [DIR]
1050 NEXT DIR
```

The designations of the six directions are stored in the individual elements, and we can visualize the field DIRECTION$ as a kind of template that during the program run is placed on the actual row of our direction table:

```
1260  IF  PASSAGE  [PLAYER,DIR]<>0  TEN  PRINT
DIR$ [DIR]
```

To check, we start our program and input a few space numbers - a glance at our map will convince us that we have so far done everything correctly.

After these preparations we shall now make movement in our adventure possible.

Anyone who has played an adventure game will know that inputting a cardinal point for the purpose of progression is probably the most frequent instruction given. Therefore, as programmers, we should accommodate the player by regarding the inputting of the initial letter as adequate, thus sparing the adventurer the task of writing out the cardinal points and accordingly pressing keys several hundreds of times.

In point of fact many adventure games can be found that for movement have no routine for command decoding and need explicitly a GO WEST.

Let us first replace line 1390 in order to permit inputs to
the adventure:

```
1390 INPUT"WHAT AM I TO DO?"; ENTRY$
```

Before our program carries out any instructions of the game,
it should first check the length of the player input. If
the input is longer than two letters, it will be a question
of some action or other, otherwise the movement routines
must be checked. This first tests whether the way in the
desired direction is at all free. If it is, reference is
made to the direction table under the appropriate direction
[column] of the space in which the player happens to be and
the new space is read off and allocated to the appropriate
variable [player]. In conclusion the player is informed of
the execution of the action.

```
1080 PRINT
1400 IF LEN[EN$]>2 THEN 1500
1410 IF EN$="N"  AND  PASSAGE[PLA,1]<>0  THEN
        PLA=PASSAGE[PLA,1]: PRINT"O.K.": GOTO 1080
1420 IF   EN$="S"   AND   PA[PLA,2]<>0   THEN
        PLA=PA[PLA,2]:PRINT"O.K.":GOTO1080
1430 IF   EN$="W"   AND   PA[PLA,3]<>0   THEN
        PLA=PA[PLA,3]:PRINT"O.K.":GOTO1080
1440 IF   EN$="E"   AND   PA[PLA,4]<>0   THEN
        PLA=PA[PLA,4]:PRINT"O.K.":GOTO1080
1450 IF   EN$="U"   AND   PA[PLA,5]<>0   THEN
        PLA=PA[PLA,5]:PRINT"O.K.":GOTO1080
1460 IF   EN$="D"   AND   PA]PLA,6]<>0   THEN
        PLA=PA[PLA,6]:PRINT"O.K.":GOTO1080
1470 PRINT"YOU CAN'T GO THAT WAY":GOTO1080
1499 REM
```

At the beginning of each game we must naturally inform the
program of the starting space:

    150 PLAYER=1

A short walk through our adventure world will now quickly
convince us that we must next tackle the matter of the
monitor picture or after a few moves our eyes will be
presented with a confused picture of little informative
value.

3.4 FORMATTING THE OUTPUT

In order to obtain a clean screen image, the screen must naturally be cleared at the start of the game:

```
1070 PRINT CHR$[147]
1080 PRINT
5000 GOTO 1070
```

Needless to say, this empty line is meaningless on an empty screen. It will always be essential after execution of a command, since our input and any communications that may have been given must be on separate lines. We achieve this scrolling by PRINTing into the last line on the screen; it is necessary at a conclusion to any move in the game.

For our inputs we will use the lowest line. The question now facing us is how after outputting the information to the player in the top third of the screen we get to the last line.

The Commodore 64 offers us two possibilities. We could for example use the cursor control commands. We could move the cursor down a suitable number of lines, but unfortunately this difference is dependent on the amount of information output, that is the number of objects, and this value is not readily available during the game.

What we need is the "PRINT AT position" command, a command that in addition to the data to be printed allows for the exact output position on the screen. Apparently our 64 lets us down here. In actual fact it offers us the same possibility as the IBM - PC or other 16-bit computers. It

is true, we do not find it in the Commodore Basic, but it
nevertheless exists, the so-called LOCATE command. This
command positions the cursor at the required point before a
PRINT operation. This is done by specifying the row and
column, then positioning the cursor at that location.

Our BASIC interpreter must during a screen output naturally
known exactly where the cursor is and for this purpose has
two storage points reserved for holding this data. We shall
make use of this feature by seeing that the very data we
want is found by the interpreter at addresses 214 for the
row and address 211 for the column. Then we use a
subroutine in the interpreter to position the cursor at the
point required.

```
1390  POKE 214, 24 :  POKE 211, 0 :  SYS 58732 :
      INPUT "What am I to do?"; ENTRY$
```

Our input is accordingly made in line 24, and the ensuring
RETURN will push the entire contents of the screen one line
up. For this reason no further measures have to be taken
for communicating the messages to the player.

Unfortunately all outputs are at the moment made in the
lowest line on the screen, but the space descriptions must
start at the top of the screen.

```
1130 POKE 214,0 :  POKE 211,0 :  SYS 58732
```

It will of course not be quite so easy for us to inform the
adventurer of the free exits, since the procedure we have
used so far does not allow for more than three exits to be
output on the screen.

No word should go beyond the end of the line. The various cardinal points should be separated by a comma, and the sentence be ended with a period.

Let us first alter line 1260

        1260 IF PASSAGE [PLA, DIR]=0 THEN GOTO 1310

and let us base our further considerations on the following example:

        I MAY PROCEED NORTH, SOUTH, EAST, UP, DOWN.

The first exit presents no difficulty for us; it can be printed out without any preliminary work. We have only to distinguish this first output from all further outputs, which is easily done. Thus the direction statement must always appear after "I may proceed" at the fourteenth printing position. Therefore:

        1270   IF   POS[0]=14   THEN   PRINT   DIR$[DIR];
        : GOTO 1310

In the case of the following direction statements however we must first carry out a test. It is important to know whether we are writing beyond the end of the line. Should this not be the case, we first print a comma and then the next cardinal point:

        1280   IF   POS[0]+LEN[DI$[DIR]] < 37   THEN
        PRINT", ":DIR$[DIR];   : GOTO 1310

Should the total length of output become greater than 37, a comma and the selection of the next line are output by means of a PRINT command:

```
1290   IF POS[0]+LEN[DI$[DIR] ] > = 37  THEN
PRINT ", " PRINT DI$[DIR];:GOTO 1310
```

With that the line in our example would be print "DOWN" on the next line. This direction statement lies in a line range not yet interrogated by our conditions. A typical feature of this range is that it must have a printing position greater than two and smaller than sixteen:

```
1300   IF POS[0]< 16 AND POS[0] >2 THEN PRINT   ",":
DIR$ [DIR];:GOTO 1310
```

With these four lines we have covered all possibilities. The final period is in any case necessary only once and is therefore placed after leaving the loop:

```
1310 NEXT DIR
1320 PRINT"."
```

Perhaps we need to explain why we need test the line length only up to 37 when after all a screen line goes from 0 to 39. You will find the answer both in line 1320 and in the comma in 1280.

3.5 GOLD, SILVER, AND OTHER USEFUL THINGS

A walk through our adventure world so far will have given
the adventurer an impression of great desolation in a scene
devoid of all interest, for after all no objects of any kind
necessary to the plot are available to him.   Likewise with
the best will in the world pure descriptions of places will
not permit a game.   Therefore let us take our map again and
enrich our world with the objects required, generally
restricting ourselves to objects important to the game.
Finally we have to ensure that everything the player finds
can be picked up and examined by him.   None the less we
cannot avoid placing at least one object in each space,
since it is very doubtful that the adventurer sees nothing
at all.   If our imagination is not sufficient, the object
concerned need be nothing in particular, a formula we so
often find in adventure games because it reduces the amount
of work involved, since in a normal woods trees, bushes,
grass, insects, etc. really are nothing in particular.

Often however even unnecessary things cannot be dispensed
with, especially when they are part of the scene and the
adventure is to give a realistic impression.

Thus we too shall have to put trees in our woods, although
the plot does not necessitate them.   In space 2, which
already lies near the mountain range, a number of lumps of
rock strengthen the impression of reality. Furthermore a
mine calls for a shack, regardless of whether it is the mine
owner's abode or a tool shed.   Finally we must also hide the
treasure somewhere or other.   In addition a number of
objects more likely to harm the player than be of use to him
are indicated.

Therefore in what follows I will put in more concrete form the plot I have in mind and select the objects required.

3.6 GOLD FEVER: THE PLOT

Version 1 sets the player the task of finding two treasures, pieces of gold and silver coins, in the area surrounding the mine. At the beginning of the game the player is supposed to be in the woods and first has to move his way forward to the mine. On his way he discovers a hole in the ground with a heavy iron chest lying at the bottom. The chest contains the silver, but unfortunately it is secured to a heavy iron chain with a padlock and the key cannot be found anywhere. At the entrance to the mine however there are a number of iron bars strong enough to break the chain or burst the lock. We can also let the player try using an explosive by letting him find dynamite in a wooden hut, a good opportunity for us to program a premature end for him. We deposit the pieces of gold in a rock cave inhabited to the player's dismay by a wild bear. The player will not however know this until he explores the cave. Should his greed for the yellow metal win and lead him to act fast, the bear, being hungry, will lose his fear of man, this, after the dynamite, being the second trap set for the adventure.

On the other hand we all know that bears simply love honey, so let's place a jar of it on a shelf in the hut. When the player, armed with the

honey, enters the cave, the bear will smell it and
disappear with the jar into the depths of the
cave.   Then nothing more stands in the way of a
successful end to this miniadventure.

The map to our adventure would now probably look something
like this:

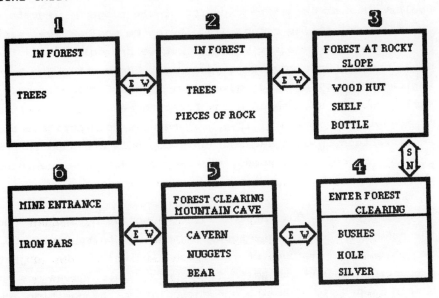

Before we complete our adventure by programming the objects,
we must give some further preliminary thought to the matter.

To enable the player to get the feel of our computer world,
the descriptions of this world will not consist of dry
nouns, but we shall keep the player's interest alive with
graphic portrayals.   The statement "I see a bear" does, it
is true, allow the player to play the adventure, but the

statement "I see an extremely-ferocious looking bear" will
on the other hand enable him to participate in our
adventure.

Now if it is the player's endeavor to find a new friend, an
input such as "Stroke the extremely ferocious-looking bear"
would, it is true, be easy enough for us as programmers to
realize, but could not be expected of the player. Therefore
in addition to its actual description we shall give each
object a reference name. In this way we are able to fix the
word length of our adventure as needed. Presumably you have
noticed that professional adventures in the English-speaking
world usually require only the first three or four letters
to identify an action. If your game uses both capitals and
small letters, please see that only capitals are used in the
case of the reference names, as these contractions are later
checked for uniformity with the player's inputs.

These two fields, OB$ for the object description and RN$ for
the reference names, are supplemented by a third field, OB,
in which the number of the space in which the object
concerned happens to be in is stored. This gives us a
simple means of checking and manipulating the position of
each object. So long as any particular object is not
actively participating in the game, OB =0, otherwise the
contents of OB correspond to the value of the variable
PLAYER or equal -1 if the adventurer is carrying the object
with him.

The following DATA lines contain all the objects essential
to the program [Gold Fever, version 1]. The figure at the
end of each line indicates in what space the object is
located at the start of the program. The quotation marks

are essential only if a comma is needed in the description of the object itself.

```
300 REM
301 DATA "LOTS OF BIG TREES", "TRE",1
302 DATA "LOTS OF BIG TREES","TRE",2
303 DATA "SEVERAL PIECES OF ROCK",ROC,2
304 DATA "AN OLD WOODEN HUT",HUT,3
305 DATA "A DIRTY JAR", "JAR",0
306 DATA "HONEY", "HON", 0
307 DATA "DATA A WOODEN BOX", "BOX",3
308 DATA "A SHELF", "SHE",0
309 DATA "SOME EXPLOSIVES", "EXP",0
310 DATA "A HOLE IN THE GROUND", "HOL", 0
311 DATA "A RUSTY IRON CHEST", "CHE",0
312 DATA "*SILVER COINS*", "SIL", 0
313 DATA "A CAVE", "CAV",5
314 DATA "A FEROCIOUS LOOKING BEAR", "BEA",0
315 DATA "LOTS OF SMALL BUSHES", "BUS", 4
316 DATA "SEVERAL IRON BARS", "BAR",6
317 DATA "*NUGGETS*", "NUG", 5
```

Exactly as in the case of the space descriptions we must also determine the number of objects before initializing the variables for object descriptions [OB$], reference names [RN$], and positions [OB]:

```
120 AC=17
190 DIM SP$[NS],PA[NS,6],OB$[AO],RN$[AO],OB[AO]
830 FOR OB= 1 TO AO
835 READ OB$[OB],RN$[OB],OB[OB]
840 NEXT
```

To store all the objects, 17 subscripted variables are
necessary, the storage location for these being provided by
the DIMensioning instruction in line 190.

How do we make the arrangement of a space visible to the
player? Well, quite simply: the variable PLAYER contains
the number of the space entered, while OB[] contains the
space numbers of the respective objects. Using a loop, for
all objects, we test whether this position number is the
same as the actual space number:

```
1160 PRINT "I SEE ";
1170 FOR I=1 TO AO
1180 IF OB[I]<>PLAYER THEN 1210
1190 IF POS[0]+LEN[OB$[I]+2] <  =39 THEN PRINT
OB$[I]:", ";:GOTO 1210
1210 NEXT I
1230 PRINT
```

Program line 1180 tests each object to see whether it is in
a space other than the one in which the player happens to
be. If this test proves to be positive, the next object is
immediately checked, otherwise the object description
concerned is output in line 1190. The semicolon ensures
that a new output will be on the same line. WE now add:

```
1200 IF POS[0]+LEN[OB$[I]+2> 39 THEN PRINT :  GOTO
1190
```

Before the next object is output, the total length of the
printout is calculated. If by printing the object
description, the comma, and the blank between two objects
[therefore +2] the cursor were to reach a position greater

than column 39, a line feed would be triggered. Then the program branches to line 1190 again, the condition is fulfilled, and the description is printed out. The comma behind the last object however is unsightly, so we move the cursor two positions to the left and print a period.

```
1220 PRINT CHR$[157];CHR$[157];"."
```

In order to obtain the screen structure of the original American adventures, we still need a separating line and another blank line:

```
1010 BLANK$="
                 "
1230 PRINT BLANK$
1330 PRINT "---------------------------------"
```

A final problem will be found after several inputs. The communications within the lower half of the screen keep on traveling up and after a few moves get mixed up with the descriptions of the environment. Before the communications are output it is the job of the program to erase the uppermost lines. This can be done by printing an adequate number of blank lines:

```
1090 POKE 211,0:POKE 214,0: SYS 58732
1100 FOR LINE=1 TO 10
1110 PRINT BLANK$
1120 NEXT LINE
```

Before we now program the actual game and occupy ourselves with the actions in the program not visible to a player, we must quickly input the additional verbs necessary for such

actions.   In addition to a series of verbs that are always
required, such as Examine, Take, Discard, the additional
verbs will depend on the contents of the adventure
concerned.   The implementation is carried out according to
the word length determined for the adventure:

```
130 AV=7
200 REM ----------------------------- VERBS
201 DATA EXAMINE
201 DATA TAKE
203 DATA DROP
204 DATA OPEN
205 DATA USE
206 DATA DESTROY
207 DATA LIGHT
810 FOR I=1 TO AV
815 READ VERS$[I]
820 NEXT I
```

We can also make the picture more attractive with a few
additions.   Different colors will help us to differentiate
between the diverse communications sent during the game.   I
have decided on a black background on which the principal
character's communications to us are output in light blue
and our inputs are made in white. Naturally you are free to
use other control codes, according to your taste.

```
10 PRINT CHR$[147]
11 POKE 53280, 12:POKE 53281, 11
12 PRINT CHR$[154]
1330 PRINT CHR[5]:"--------------------------------
--------------"
```

```
1390 POKE 211,0:POKE 214,24:SYS 58732:PRINTCHR$(5);
:INPUT "WHAT AM I TO DO"; EN$:PRINTCHR$(155);
```

We have thus reached the external form described in the first chapter of this book and will now establish the playing performance of our program.

3.7 ANALYSIS OF THE INPUTS

Changes in direction required by the player, a group of commands with word lengths of one or two letters, are already being recognized and correctly executed. The standard input however always consists of a verb and an object, the word lengths, apart form the minimum word length necessary for recognition of the terms, are not being subject to any restrictions. In order to be able to react as required by the player, our program must check his input:

Has the verb used been programmed?
Has the object been provided for?

If both questions can be answered in the affirmative, the input is broken down into a verb and an object and the verb and object numbers are determined; if the costituent parts of the input are not defined, an appropriate communication is output to the adventurer.

3.7.1 STRING MANIPULATION

The essential difference between a computer and a programmed pocket calculator is the ability of the computer to deal with texts. Naturally a computer has no understanding of texts, but interprets them as a collection of specific characters, what is known as a character string. Strings are generally combinations of all characters that can be input via a keyboard. The computer provides a series of functions for manipulating these character strings.

In the case of our Commodore 64 these functions include not only a series of conversion commands such as VAL[] and STR$[] that converts a figure into a string or a string into a figure, but also the commands LEFT$, RIGHT$, and MID$.

These three functions provide a precisely defined partial string out of the total character string for further processing by the program. Thus the function LEFT$["ABCDEF",3] produces a string comprising the three lefthand characters, that is the substring ABC. Therefore the character string to be processed and the number of letters required must, as necessary parameters, first be transmitted with the input function. The same applies to RIGHT$. MID$[X$, S, X], beginning with position S, provides us with a string X characters long of X$. Thus for example our adventure program will ascertain the positions of the blank character between verb and object and then with LEFT$ and RIGHT$ ascertain these from the player's INPUT$. In order to calculate the number of letters necessary, the total length of the input must first be ascertained with LEN[INPUT$].

If an input is not executed in lines 1290 to 1340, it is assumed, if the length of the input is less than three letters. that an input error has been made. Since "No exit leads there!" has been output, a new move by the player begins.

If a longer input is involved, the program run is continued with line 2000:

```
1470 IF  LEN(ENTRY$) < 3 THEN PRINT"YOU CAN'T GO
THAT WAY!":GOTO1080
2000 LN=LEN(ENTRY$)
2010 FOR EL=1 TO LN
2020 TEST$=MID$(ENTRY$,EL, 1)
2030 IF TEST$<>" " THEN NEXT EL
```

When the length of the total input has been ascertained,
each letter beginning from the left, is checked using a loop
to see whether it is a space. When the space character is
found, the length of the verb is established [previously
checked character minus 1] and the verb can be allocated to
the variable EV$. After the remaining length has been
ascertained, the object can be transferred to the variable
EO$.

If a "one-word command" was used [HELP], the residual length
will be less than zero. Since no object has to be provided
for further processing, branching is made direct [line 2060]
to verb analysis [line 2090]:

```
2040 EV$=LEFT$(ENTRY$,3)
2050 RL = LN-EL
2060 IF RL<0 THEN 2090
2070 EO$=RIGHT$(ENTRY$,RL)
2080 EO$=LEFT$(EO$,3)
2090 FOR VN=1 TO AV
2100 IF EV$=VERB$(VN) THEN 2130
2110 NEXT VN
```

Within the loop the text of the first word input is compared
with the verbs that are possible in the game. If an
identical string is found, the loop index corresponds to the

verb number and the loop is exited.   If the loop has been
completely exhausted and no identity found,   this means that
the   programmer   did not provide the verb concerned.   The
player is informed of this:

```
2120   PRINT  "I DO NOT UNDERSTAND   THE   VERB!":GOTO
1080
```

The   object   number   is   then   ascertained   using   the   same
principle:

```
2130 FOR N=1 TO AO
2140 IF EO$=RN$[N] THEN 5000
2150 NEXT N
2160 PRINT "I DO NOT KNOW THIS OBJECT!" :GOTO 1080
```

By   creating these lines,   we have put a substantial part of
our development work behind us.   The above routines ensures
that   the   screen is attractively structured,   just as   they
also create "understanding" for the player's input.

They   ascertain which of the possible verbs   the   adventurer
has used and with which object he would like to do something
with.   This makes it possible to branch the program sequence
to   a   program line provided for execution of   the   action
concerned.   Because of these central control tasks this part
of the program is also called DRIVER.

3.8 SUMMARY: PROGRAM STRUCTURE

It now becomes clear that our adventure programs consist essentially of three parts:

1. The adventure data
2. The adventure driver
3. The execution of the moves in the game

1. The data used as a basis for the game is transferred to the work variables at the start of the program.

2. The control of the entire program sequence falls to the driver. The driver structures the screen output, takes over the player's inputs, evaluates them, and initiates the execution of the commands. It is independent of the particular adventure concerned and is used in all adventures.

3. The third part of the program is the actual adventure. If all the conditions necessary to a plot are fulfilled, the action concerned is carried out.

In order to maintain a perspective, the structure of our test adventures is represented schematically, the line numbers available are also specified.

INITIALIZATION

100 200   CONTROL VARIABLE INITIALIZATION

200 300   VERBS

300 500   OBJECT DESCRIPTION AND POSITION OF OBJECT

500 600   ROOM DESCRIPTION

900 1000 OTHER VARIABLE INITIALIZATION

ADVENTURE MOVEMENT

1000 1070 DIRECTION INITIALIZATION

1080 1330 SCREEN SETUP

1390   PLAYER'S INPUT

1400 1500 MOVE PLAYER

2000 3000 ANALYZE INPUT

EXECUTION

5000 30000 MOVES

For the extensions to be provided later there are enough unused line numbers available in the individual blocks.

We shall see how this concept can easily be extended to an adventure interpreter or used for realizing graphic adventures.

Thus we shall be able to use the driver almost unchanged and have only to modify the remaining parts of the program.

3.9 WHEN CAN ACTIONS BE PERFORMED?

Let us now visualize the player who wants to find our two
treasures. At a glance he establishes that he is in the
middle of a woods, surrounded by trees and lumps of rock.
As a proficient adventure player or reader of the previous
chapters, he knows that what he is looking for can lie
hidden in the most inconcpicuous or commonplace things.

How will he react?
What inputs must we expect?

In all probability he will try to proceed with instructions
such as EXAMINE WOOD, EXAMINE TREE, or EXAMINE LUMPS OF
ROCK.

TAKE TREE is less probable, but nevertheless, in order to
take the wind out of the sails of all critics of our
programs, we must program a statement such as "I am not that
strong." In addition there are many statements that show
that an input really was understood and encourage the player
to go on playing.

Understandably, if the result of every second or third input
were a "I do not know what you mean!", there would be a very
great inducement to switch the computer off.

Therefore in the case of spaces 1 and 2, because we have not
provided for any action here, but only want to make our
world bigger, we shall provide only for the output of
various messages to the player, a task quickly dealt with by
a print command. However, after the player has entered
space 3 and discovered the wooden hut, he will take a close

look at this and at the same time discover the shelf with
the jar.   Naturally, in addition to the shelf and the hut,
the jar must appear in the description of the scene ["I see
input TAKE JAR could give us more headaches: the jar that
has just appeared must now disappear.   It cannot go back to
its old place, for when our player makes an INVENTORY, it
too must of course be listed.

During the course of play the player cannot examine the jar
in space 1 or space 2.   In general all inputs relating to
the jar should be answered in the negative so long as the
jar is not in the immediate vicinity of the player.

This however is a matter of taste that lies within the
programmer's discretion, since he may hold the view that in
reality the jar has stood on the shelf untouched since time
immemorial and that the player has not yet seen it.

If however the player is compelled by the many surprises
held in an adventure when he starts all over again, he knows
the starting position of various objects and one can readily
make it possible for him to take them, even though they were
not listed in the line "I see ...".

Actually the process of taking is made even easier to
program as a result. Finally there is one more condition to
check, but we will do like most adventure producers and let
only visible objects be available.

Thus the wooden hut cannot be examined by our principal
character unless it is within reach. We shall not discover
the honey until we have picked up the jar and opened it.

Before any command is executed, all these conditions must first be checked to see whether they are correct. Even our short adventure with only six spaces will accordingly necessitate many program lines. If we consider only the verbs introduced at this stage of the development [examine, take, discard, open, use, destroy] and our seventeen objects, we already have to program actions for 102 different player inputs. If we were to enter all the program lines without any special structure one after the other, it would be easy to explain very long program execution times. Therefore we shall now split up into several blocks, the part of the program to be produced.

In principal there are two possibilities open to us. In one case we could reserve a sufficient number of program lines for each space and reserve a few statements there for every possible action taken by the player. This technique is chosen very often and also has the advantage, owing to the direct execution of a command, which of course does not have to be prepared beforehand in any way, that it is very fast and above all that a very clear program is produced, a program that can be conveniently and easily extended or edited without reference to any lists. Should you ever want to occupy yourself with this execution of an adventure program, the following realization of our space 1 should suffice as a stimulus. Note that it is an example that has nothing to do with our concept. Therefore please do not overwrite any of the lines in the program we have so far produced.

```
10   REM EXAMPLE ----DO NOT ENTER THESE LINES
100  INPUT "WHAT SHALL I DO";ENTRY$
200  REM
300  ON SP GOTO 1000,2000,3000,4000,5000,6000
1000 PRINT CHR$[147]:REM ROOM 1
1010 PRINT "I AM IN THE WOOD!"
1020 PRINT "I SEE LOTS OF BIG TREES"
1040 REM
1100 PRINT "I CAN GO SOUTH,EAST"
1200 IF ENTRY$="S" THEN ROOM=6:GOTO100
1210 IF ENTRY$="E" THEN ROOM=2:GOTO100
1260 IF LEN[ENTRY$]<3 THEN PRINT "YOU CAN'T GO
     THAT WAY"
1300 IF ENTRY$="INV" OR "INVENTORY" THEN 200
1400 IF VE$="EXA" AND OB$="TRE" THEN PRINT"I SEE
     NOTHING SPECIAL":GOTO100
1410 IF VE$="TAU" AND OB$="TRE" THEN PRINT"I'M NOT
     THAT STRONG":GOTO100
1999 PRINT"I DO NOT UNDERSTAND WHAT YOU
     MEAN":GOTO100
2000 REM ROOM2
3000 REM ROOM3
```

If you have had a look at the above lines or even input them
into your C64, you will find that a workable adventure can
be created in a very simple way and you will perhaps ask
yourself why we have not used this concept, seeing that it
can be understood without lengthy comments.

On the one hand, very involved adventures require far more
memory, for it is not possible for us avoid listing
identical routines several times, since, sticking to a known
example, we should have to be able to deposit the jar in

every space [six identical program lines], not forgetting
that we should also have to be able to take it again.   In
our adventure system all of two program lines are used, in
contrast to these twelve.   That alone should be enough to
quickly invalidate the argument of clarity and editing
friendliness.

Imagine if as an extension to the adventure further jars are
needed to continue the plot, for this or some other reason
we prefer to make a small wooden barrel out of the jar.   If
at this point your adventure already had forty spaces, you
may now make "Take barrel" out of "Take jar" in the
corresponding number of lines.   The same applies to "Discard
jar", "Open jar", etc. If on the other hand you have stuck
to our adventure system, you simply alter line 305 and there
you are!

Let us forget this method and come back to our adventure.
We let the plot unfold in precisely defined program lines,
but now each block contains the treatment of one verb.

Our driver has already established the verb and object
numbers.   Therefore we can specifically transfer these
blocks.   Thus the sensible thing to do is to assign program
lines beginning with 5000 to all lines used in the execution
of the command "Examine", the action "Take" accordingly
being realized from line 6000.

The program sequence is controlled by the adventure driver
with the aid of the verb number in line 2200:

        2200 ON VN GOTO 5000,6000,7000,8000,9000,10000

With program line 5000 the block EXAMINE now begins.   It is
easy to see that it is here that the greatest amount of work
is asked of us.

It is not only that after EXAMINE but the message   "IN THE
HUT THERE IS AN OLD SHELF" must be output and the shelf must
appear as a variable object.   Now, we must also make sure
that the hut is available at the space just visited and, if
necessary, must send a communication such as "I DO NOT SEE
ANYTHING LIKE THAT HERE" to the player.

These considerations already show the work involved in
adventure programming.   Fortunately however many different
player inputs can be answered by one and the same program
line.

Thus the program part dealing with the player's examining
actions will first check whether the object on which further
information is required is within the player's reach and
accordingly in the same space or even in his possession,
otherwise the input of the next move can be started at once:

```
5000 IF OB[N] <>PL AND OB[N] <> - 1 THEN GOTO 5900
5900 REM OBJECT NOT PRESENT
5904?"I KNOW THAT OBJECT":GOTO 1080
5990 PRINT "I  DO NOT  SEE  ANYTHING  LIKE  THAT
HERE!": GOTO 1080
```

3.10 THE CONDITIONS

Apart from two conditions previously mentioned, a number of other prerequisites can be formulated without which it will not be possible to realize an adventure:

    Object is in the space
    Object is being carried by the player
    Object is not in the space
    Flag is set
    Flag is not set
    Player is in a specific space

As we shall see later, this list does not claim to be complete. It is conceivable for example that the last condition may be inverted or that certain actions cannot be executed in a particular space, but probably in every other space.

The flags that have cropped up at this point need explanation. These are signal switches that we want to realize by means of a further field, but these field variables must not be able to assume more than two states: either a flag is set, in which case the contents of the variables must be -1, or it is not set, which must correspond to a zero. These flags are used in our adventure to identify certain states:

    Is a door open or closed?
    Was an obstacle removed or not?
    Is a monster to put an end to the player's doings
    or may the player carry on?

In the practice however the formulation of a single condition will not usually suffice to classify the situation unequivocally, so logical interconnections of several conditions become necessary in order to ensure that certain actions are not carried out haphazardly and at the wrong times.

These logical operations will be AND or OR operations. In the case of our adventure practice this means that either both [AND] or only the one or the other [OR] of two or more interconnections have to be fulfilled. If we cannot dispense with more than two conditions, bracketing will usually be imperative. An example will make this clear:

Let us think about the explosive in our box. It is intended to be used in the case of over-hasty players to spoil the pleasure they derive from getting done fast. For reasons of fairness however a warning of the risk of explosion is perfectly appropriate, so following "Examine explosive" the statement "It looks very explosive" must be output. If the player then still tries to take the explosive, he himself is to blame for his end.

If the player has actually made the above input, the driver will make the numbers 1 [examine] and 9 [explosive] available. The problem that now faces us is that we cannot rest content with checking a space, for we must not forget that the player, it is true, is not able to pick up the explosive and take it with him, but can pick up the box and take it with him, and if he takes the box with him, he

has the explosive as well with him. Let us
therefore check whether the player meant to take
the explosive AND at the same time whether the
wooden box [object number 7] is in the space just
visited OR in the adventure's inventory. The
actual object in the plot [number 9] is not
available. Therefore after line 5000, the program
sequence is continued with line 5908.

Therefore the execution of the command "Examine
explosive" must be formulated as follows:

```
5904   IFN=9AND[OB[7]=PLOR OB[7]=-1]THEN PRINT  "IT
       LOOKS VERY EXPLOSIVE!": GOTO 1080
```

3.11 THE ACTIONS

The previous example has made the execution of the simple action, the output of a communication to the player, clear to us.

Usually however this print command is only an accessory to other actions, such as manipulations of OB[], used as feedback to give the adventurer confirmation of the execution of the command.

Commands such as TAKE, DROP, DESTROY, and OPEN always mean a change of location for an object. Either the object is taken by the player along with him or goes into the inventory of a particular space. Perhaps it disappears completely from the game. Just imagine the amazement of the person playing Gold Fever if the bear has obviously eaten the honey, but the full jar can still be found somewhere!

Another, frequently required action is the setting or resetting of the previously mentioned flags in order to create the prerequisites for later actions.

We must not forget any conditional changes in location of the player initiated by magic or harmless actions. A subsequent extension to Gold Fever could make a gigantic maze of passages out of the bear's cave, and after "Examine cave" the player finds himself in the middle of the cave, even though he has not entered the cave by a movement in the direction of the appropriate cardinal point. The increased amount of programming work however will make our adventure only more realistic, for how is one supposed to explore a cave thoroughly without entering it?

As with the conditions, we can compile a list of possible
actions in this case, but such a list cannot claim to be
complete. It does however provide an adequate basis, and it
is possible to write good adventures with just the
conditions and actions presented.

        Output communication to the player
        Object disappears
        Object comes into the inventory
        Object reappears in the space
        Flag is set
        Flag is deleted
        Player is transferred to another space

3.12 PROGRAMMING THE EXECUTION OF THE COMMANDS

Below you will find information on various special features
that have to be observed in the case of some particular
commands. I shall explain only a few typical program lines.
Please obtain the remaining lines from the listing of the
miniversion of Gold Fever at the end of this chapter.

3.12.1 ACTION: EXAMINE

First it is an established fact that the result of examining
an object is always communicated in the form of a sentence.

Often it will be one and the same sentence [I see nothing in
particular], for which reason we do not output the
communications direct to the player in such cases, but
allocate the text at the start of the program to a variable
and in due course print out its contents.

Since we have only 80 characters available for a BASIC line
and have also to formulate the conditions in the line
concerned, we shall sometimes not be able to avoid preparing
a number of messages that are needed only once.

```
600   REM ------------------- COMMUNICATIONS
601   MS$[1]="I CANNOT SEE ANYTHING IN PARTICULAR".
602   MS$[2]="I AM NOT THAT STRONG".
603   MS$[3]="WHAT DO YOU MEAN?"
604   MS$[4]="THE BEAR TAKES THE HONEY AND"
605   MS$[5]="DISAPPEARS  INTO THE DEPTHS  OF  THE
CAVE".
```

Line 5000 has already been explained. By checking the value in OB[], it ensures that the actual object concerned is in the player's vicinity.

If this is so, the program line appropriate to this object is ascertained from the object number N. If all the conditions programmed there have been fulfilled, the rest of the line is exhausted and the program then continues with the rest of the screen image:

```
5002 IF N=1 THEN PRINT MS$[1]: GOTO 1080
5003 IF N=3 THEN PRINT MS$[1]: GOTO 1080
5004 IF N=4 THEN PRINT "IN A CORNER THERE IS A
SHELF". :OB[8]=PL: GOTO 1080
```

On examining the wooden hut [N=4] the player discovers the shelf. This was in space 0, the storeroom, and is now positioned in the player's space, so in lines 1170 to 1210 the adventure driver outputs, among other things, "a shelf".

As in the case of the shelf, however, it is conceivable that an object may turn up that is afterwards taken by the player.

Then a formulation as in 5004 would no longer be adequate, as in the event of any further examination of the shelf the jar would automatically be taken out of the inventory and put back in the space.

We can avoid this mistake only if we first make sure that the jar has not yet been in the game and accordingly is still in the storeroom.

```
5008 IF N=8 AND OB(5)=0 THEN PRINT "ON THE
     SHELF THERE IS A JAR.":OB(5)=PL
     :GOTO 1080
5009 IF N=8 AND OB(5)<>0 THEN PRINT MS$(
     1):GOTO 1080
```

In all further examinations of the shelf the player will not
find anything else in particular [line 5009].

A further example will show the use of the flags.   When the
player has found the treasure chest,   he will see that it is
secured with an iron chain.   After he has removed this
obstacle,   the chest must of course be opened before the
valuable contents can be seen.   To make these three states
clear to the player,   it would be possible to introduce
further objects, such as a chest secured with an iron chain,
an unsecured chest, and an open chest.   This very great
volume of programming work,   which incidentally of course
restricts the storage location available,   can be avoided by
using signal switches.   It would be sensible of you to draw
up a table during the construction of your adventure,   so
that you really do set the correct flags:

Flag	0	−1
1	Chain intact	Chain destroyed
2	Chest closed	Chest open

You may now ask: Why of all values we use   [−1] and not
another value? Or why not only one flag with various figures
for every possible state?

71

The reason is we make use of the fact that in the case of
the BASIC interpreter a TRUTH is always represented by a −1,
so in the IF statements we do not have to specify any
comparative values:

        IF FL[1]=−1 corresponds to   IF FL[1]
        IF FL[1]=0 corresponds to   IF NOT FL[1]

Accordingly the following lines apply to our example:

        5011 IFN=11ANDNOTFL[1] THENPRINT"IT IS
               SECURED WITH AN IRON CHAIN.":GOTO 1080
        5012 IF N=11ANDFL[1]ANDNOTFL[2]THENPRINT
               "I CAN'T SEE ANYTHING FROM THE
               OUTSIDE.": GOTO 1080
        5013 IF N=11ANDFL[1]ANDFL[2]THENPRINT"IT
               IS FULL OF SILVER COINS.":OB[12]=PLG:
               GOTO 1080

A further point to which we must pay special attention finds
its justification in the layout of our word analysis.

The completely identical objects 1 and 2 form part of the
equipment of the first two spaces.   When the input of the
game is checked, it will never be possible to ascertain any
other object number than a 1, which number, in the event
that the player is located in space 2, does not correspond
to the facts.

In order to be able to acknowledge input errors correctly,
we used line 5901, which now enables us to handle these
special cases.

Thus we solve the problem "Examine trees" for space 2 in the following manner:

```
5901 IF N=1 AND PL=2 THEN PRINT MS$[1]:GOTO 1080
5910 IFN=1ANDPL=5ANDOB[14]=5THENPRINT "I SEEM TO
     WHET HIS APPETITE.":GOTO 1080
```

To conclude the routine, we must provide a last line executed without any condition if none of the conditions was fulfilled in any of the preceding program lines. With this undefined game inputs are intercepted and, if no applicable condition is found, we prevent the lines of the other verbs from being exhausted and accordingly prevents the program from getting out of control. Even if we forget an action that is not necessary to the development of the adventure, a player will never notice this:

```
5990  PRINT "I DO NOT SEE ANYTHING LIKE THAT
      HERE!" :  GOTO 1080
```

3.12.2 ACTION: TAKE

Exactly as the player can examine only an object that is near him, he will not be able to take such an object unless it is either in the same space as the player or in his pocket.

```
6000 IF OB[N]<> PL AND OB[N]<>-1 THEN GOTO 6900
```

Accordingly it would be quite simple to execute this command, but with a few objects we should deny the adventurer his wish.

Thus we should allow for this fact that a completely full iron chest is presumably too heavy for only one person. Likewise we cannot ignore even stupid attempts on the part of the player such as "Take tree."

```
6001 IF N=1 THEN PRINT MS$[2]:GOTO 1080
6005 IF N=11 THEN PRINT MS$[2]:GOTO 1080
```

Naturally things can get even worse, for we must of course set a sufficient number of traps for the player, so that victory is not made too easy for him. Thus according to our script touching the explosive should lead to an explosion and accordingly end the game. The same applies if the player tries to seize the nuggets without first offering the bear a tidbit. It would be equally fatal for the player to attempt to take the bear:

```
6015   IF  N=1 AND PL=5 THEN  MS$[0]="THE  BEAR  HAS
         KILLED ME.":GOTO 4500
6018 IF N=17 AND NOT PL[3] THEN MS$[0]="THE BEAR IS
         ATTACKING ME.":GOTO 4500
6900   IF  N=9  THEN MS$[0]="IT EXPLODED WHEN I TOUCHED
         IT!":GOTO 4500
```

Note: In line 4500 a routine begins that is called up when
the game is lost. MS$[0] is provided is this routine for an
explanatory message.

Flag 3 is set when the bear is in possession of the honey.

If there is nothing to stop the player enriching himself
with any of the objects used in our adventure, we have only
to allocate the new place number, a -1, to the object:

```
6010 IF N=5 THEN OB[5]=-1:PRINT"O.K.":GOTO 1080
```

3.12.3 ACTION: DISCARD

Some time or other the player will want to get rid of these objects, either because we as programmers have limited his carrying capacity or because he wants to use them in some way or other.

In practice the "Discard" routine hardly raises any problems. Over and above that it is convincing in its shortness, for the only prerequisite is that the object to be discarded is in the player's possession, which is tested in line 7005 in respect of all objects:

```
7005  IF  OB[N]<>-1 THEN PRINT"BUT I DON'T  HAVE
ANYTHING LIKE THAT.":GOTO 1080
7900 OB[N]=PL:PRINT"O.K.":GOTO 1080
```

Mistakes made by the player are immediately recognized and accordingly acknowledged. If the object was in the inventory, a new location is allocated to it with an alteration of the contents of OB[].

In principal these two lines are enough, but it may be necessary to carry out further reactions in addition to the position change. Thus in Gold-Fever we arranged for the bear to take the jar and disappear with it into the depths of the cave. Naturally this action must be carried out only if the player happens to be in space 5. At all other spaces the operation is likewise executed by line 7900.

```
7020 IFN=5ANDPL=5 THEN OB[5]=0:FL[3]=- 1:
PRINTWS$[4]:PRINTTMS$[5]:OB[14]=0:GOTO 1080
```

3.12.4 ACTION: OPEN

Right at the beginning of this program part there is the now
a known test for avoiding technical errors. Again it is
necessary to check both the space and the inventory.

```
8000 IF OB[N]<>PL AND OB[N]<>-1 THEN PRINT
"THERE IS NOTHING LIKE THAT HERE.":GOTO 1080
```

The action itself will mostly consist of setting a flag and
outputting a communication:

```
8025  IF N=11 AND FL[1] THEN PRINT"O.K.  -THE  LID
OPENS BACKWARDS."FL[2]=-1:GOTO 1080
```

We must not forget actions that are unimportant, but
possible in the situation. Our jar may again serve as an
example. A logically thinking adventurer will first want to
open it before any closer examination and would undoubtedly
be suprised if he failed to so simply because it was
unimportant to the game.

```
8010 IF N=5 THEN PRINT"O.K.":GOTO 1080
```

The end of this block ensures that not only wrong technical
inputs but also such impossible instructions as "Open honey"
are recognized.

```
8999 PRINT"I DO NOT UNDERSTAND WHAT YOU MEAN.":GOTO
1080
```

3.13 SUMMARY

I hope that the explanations given in respect to what are probably the most frequent types of action will have made the execution of the actual game programming clear to you. To summarize, it can be said that in principle the individual actions are covered by two program lines.

Thus at the beginning of a block a test is made to see whether execution of the action is possible from the technical point of view. Finally steps are take to ensure that the program is correctly continued even if there is an error.

Recognition of the prerequisites for the execution of a command, just as the action itself, is usually something that is very easily programmed and something that in the case of our adventure system has been standardized. The following list is intended to help you realism your first adventure:

CONDITION	IN THE BASIC PROGRAM
Object is in the space	OB[object]=PL
Object is being carried by the player	OB[object]=-1
Object is not in the space	OB[object]<>PL
Flag is set	FL[x]=-1
Flag is not set	FL[x]=0
Player is in a specific space	PL=space

ACTIONS   IN THE BASIC PROGRAM

Output communication to the player	PRINT"" or MS$
Object disappears	OB[object]=0
Object comes into the inventory	OB[object]=-1

CONDITION   IN THE BASIC PROGRAM

Object reappears in the space	OB[object]=PL
Flag is set	FL[x]=-1
Flag is deleted	FL[x]=0
Player is transferred to another space	PL=space

EXPLANATION OF THE MORE IMPORTANT VARIABLES:

NS	Number of spaces in an adventure
AO	Number of objects
AV	Number of verbs
PA	Ways out from a space
I	Counter in loops
N	Number of objects used
OB	Location of an object
DI	Counter for directions
PL	Player's location space
VN	Number of verb used
WL	Significant word length
EN$	Player's input
EO$	Subject of player's input
EV$	Verb of player's input
MS$	Communication to be output
OB$	Description of an object
RN$	Call name of an object
VE$	Verb

3.14 THE LAST STEPS

Before our adventure corresponds to the ideas developed in chapter 2, we must think about three further program parts.

Thus, if a game is to be played satisfactorily, it is absolutely essential to provide the player with the possibility of making a quick inventory.

It is quite possible to execute this routine in the same way as the handling of the verbs. As what is involved here is a fundamental function of the adventures, we shall supplement our driver in some suitable manner.

3.14.1 INVENTORY

Like the routines to be prepared later for storing and loading the state of the game, and inventory belongs to the group of what are called one-word commands. We have left sufficient room for this program part between program lines 1470 [end of the movement routine] and 2000 [analysis of the input].

To avoid keeping our driver occupied for an unnecessarily long time comparing each of the player's moves with the commands in this special group, we first decide whether what is involved is one of these special instructions or a normal input.

The usual input made by a player will have a length of at least seven letters. Therefore, if the length of the input is less, let us assume that it is a one-word command:

```
1490 IF LEN[ENTRY$]>6 THEN GOTO 2000
```

If the player's input is not a normal combination of a verb
and object, all the lines in which the handling of a one-
word command begins will run through in turn until agreement
of the first three letters is established.

In practice the execution of the inventory consists in
running through a simple loop that prints out on the screen
all the objects in the adventure that are marked -1:

```
1499 REM -----------START OF INVENTORY ----------
1500 IF LEFT$[ENTRY$,3]<>"INV" THEN GOTO 2000
1510 PRINT"I AM CARRYING THE FOLLOWING WITH ME:"
1520 FOR I=1 TO AO
1520 IF OB[I]=-1 THEN PRINT OB$[I]
1540 NEXT I
1550 GOTO 1080
1560 REM -----------END OF INVENTORY -----------
```

3.14.2 THE TITLES

Seen from the purely technical aspect, we have completed our
program with these lines. All required functions are
available, and nothing more stands in the way of a game.
But how long is the adventurer to wander about in our world?
When has he reached his goal?

So far as the action is concerned, the miniversion of Gold
Fever ends when both the nuggets and the silver coins are in
the player's possession.

A single BASIC line is all that is necessary in this case to prevent all further inputs and to transfer program control to a part that informs the player in some appropriate way of his success and ends the game.

```
1340 IF OB[12]=-1 AND OB[17]=-1 THEN GOTO 4800
```

Typical of adventure games however is an entirely different, less glorious end. Since players of our program will of necessity normally end their game somewhat earlier, we program a further end solution from line 4500.

In the execution of the game-ending actions we had of course already prepared a suitable message, so that the player at least does not have to be left in any doubt as to the cause of his failure.

```
4500 PRINT CHR$[147]:REM PLAYER DEAD ---
4600 PRINT "THIS IS THE END!":PRINT MS$[0]
4610 PRINT"I AM DEAD !":PRINT
4620 INPUT"SHALL I TRY AGAIN";A$
4630 IF LEFT$[A$,1]="Y" THEN RUN
4640 PRINT CHR$[147]:END
```

Here the inclusion of the individual message in ms$[0] allows us to use this for every situation and every adventure. If at all necessary, alterations will not involve much work. For this reason the above lines, just like the news of victory from 4800, may be regarded as further additions to our adventure driver.

Let us also remember that loading adventures and playing them through in a few hours is not all typical of adventures and let us finally program a normal program end.

Even though such software is on the market, it does not say much for the user friendliness of a program if the program can be left just by pressing the stop or restore keys.

Therefore let us insert a further one-word command into our system:

```
1500 IF LEFT$(ENTRY$,3)<>"INV" THEN GOTO 1950
1950 IF LEFT$(ENTRY$,3)<>"END" THEN GOTO 2000
1960  PRINT "THE AUTHOR WISHES YOU BETTER LUCK NEXT
TIME!":END
```

Logically these were the last lines of our adventure; we have realized all conceivable versions of the end of the game. But how on the other hand does the beginning of our work look?

If we start our program just as it is, its first action consists in preparing the work variables, a job that raises the thought of a program crash, especially in the case of major adventures. Then one finds oneself in the middle of the program and as inexperienced newcomer to adventure games perhaps sees the purpose of the game as arranging a sightseeing tour through an electronically simulated world.

As first impressions are important let us take the trouble of providing our program with one or, better still, several titles.

It will be the job of the first title to give some
information, in a concise but attractive form, to indicate
the title and nature of the program, and to provide some
information on the author.

We bring the next picture onto the screen before the
variables are initialized. During this period of time this
title can give some information on the task allotted to the
player and introduce him into action.

If of course establishing the task set is part of the idea
of the game, this screen will be missing and the program
title will be followed by an explanation of the idea of the
game, which otherwise must be implemented as a third
screen.

How was it when you received your first adventure and got it
into the memory? Did you know the purpose of these programs
or did you sit in front of your computer not knowing what to
do?

After all let us not forget that there will always be
beginners who are happy if the can load a program without
error messages after they have switched on the computer.

SCREEN   I

Welcome to the miniversion of GOLD FEVER

Some days ago,   while looking for
a fortune in the new world, you met a
critically ill old man to whom you gave
help in his last hours.   Out of
gratitude he told you about his gold mine
and the rest of his wealth hidden there.
Many dangers faced you on the way there;
soon you will have reached your goal and
it will be seen whether the old man was
telling the truth or talking in   a
delirium.

Do you want advice on your   further
action?

SCREEN II

                C64 - Adventure System, Version i.0
                     [c] 1984 by Walkowiak

         Imagine a robot that you can control with
         a sequence of commands.   I am this robot
         and on behalf shall expose myself to the
         dangers of the boldest of adventures.

         To enable you to make me act sensibly, I
         shall accurately describe the situation
         in which I happen to find myself at any
         given time.   Then you tell me in two
         words such as, for example, EXAMINE DOOR,
         TAKE KNIFE, what am I to do.

         Moreover I understand the commands
              INVentory   SAVE   LOAD
              VOCabularies HELP   END
              SCOre and   INStructions

                      [Press key]

In these two examples we have shown you what was meant.   In
your own adventure games program lines [10 - 100] and [700 -
900] are available for this task.

You   should incorporate the general explanations as a
subroutine, being concluded by RETURN. This permits further
extension of the adventure driver and enables the player to
recall the rules without interrupting the game.

3.15 INFORMATION ON THE PROGRAM LISTING

The next pages contain the complete listing of GOLDFEVER mini version 1.0. It should however be noted that it is not a question of additional program lines; all lines explained in the previous text are also listed.

You will see that with the techniques so far presented it is possible to develop demanding adventures that do not need to shun comparison with corresponding purchasable software.

It is now up to you whether you first put the book aside and develop an adventure game of your own or prefer to learn about other features that can make a perfect adventure from a good one.

Some of the program lines are longer than 80 characters so it will be necessary to use the abbreviations for the BASIC keywords to enter these lines [?=PRINT, N-shift-E=NEXT, etc.].

The programs in this book were listed using a TURBOPRINT/GT printer interface in the SPECIAL LISTING MODE. By using this special mode it should be easier to enter the programs. Please refer to Appendix A for a complete list of the special codes used to list the programs.

```
1 REM -- MINI-GOLD FEVER, VERSION 1.0 --
2 REM     [C] 1984 BY WALKOWIAK
10 REM ---------------------- TITLE PIC
TURE
11 POKE53281,11:POKE53280,12:PRINTCHR$[1
42]
12 PRINT"{CLR}"
13 PRINT"{CM5}                      {CM+
}{CM+}{CM+}{CM+}{CM+}{CM+}{CM+}{CM+}{CM+
}{CM+}{CM+}{CM+}{CM+}{CM+}{CM+}
14 PRINT"{YEL}    {SHO}{CMY} {SHO}{SHP} {
CMG}  {SHO}{SHM} {BLK}{SHO}{CMY} {SHO}{C
MY} {CMG}{CMM} {SHO}{CMY} {SHO}{SHP}{CM5
}{CM+}{CM+}{CM+}{CM+}{CM+}{CM+}{CM+}{CM+
}
15 PRINT"{YEL}    {CMH}{CMP} {CMH}{CMM} {
CMG}  {CMH}{CMM} {BLK}{SHL}{CMP} {SHL}{C
MP} {CMG}{CMM} {SHL}{CMP} {SHL}{SH@}{CM5
} {CMM}{CMN}{CMN} {CM+}{CM+}{CM+}
16 PRINT"{YEL}    {SHL}{SH@} {SHL}{SH@} {
SHL}{CMP} {SHL}{SHN} {BLK}{CMG}  {SHL}{C
MP} {SHM}{SHN} {SHL}{CMP} {CMH}{SHM}{CM5
} {CMM}{CMN}{CMN} {CM+}{CM+}{CM+}
17 PRINT"{BLK}    {SHU}{SH*}{SH*}{SH*}{SH*
}{SH*}{SH*}{SH*}{SH*}{SH*}{SH*}{SH*}{SH*
}{SH*}{SH*}{SH*}{SHI} {CM5}   {CM+}{CM+}{
CM+}    {CMM}{CMN}{CMN} {CM+}{CM+}{CM+}
18 PRINT"{BLK}   {SH-}    {CM8}[C] 1984
 {BLK}{SH-}{CM5}   {CM+}{CM+}{CM+}      {
CMM}{CMN}{CMN} {CM+}{CM+}{CM+}
19 PRINT"{BLK}   {SH-}       {CM8}BY
 {BLK}{SH-}{CM5}   {CM+}{CM+}{CM+}      {
CMM}{CMN}{CMN} {CM+}{CM+}{CM+}
20 PRINT"{BLK}   {SH-}   {CM8}JOERG WALKOWIA
K{BLK}{SH-}{CM5}   {CM+}{CM+}{CM+}      {
CMM}{SH@}{SHN} {CM+}{CM+}{CM+}
21 PRINT"{BLK}   {SHJ}{SH*}{SH*}{SH*}{SH*
}{SH*}{SH*}{SH*}{SH*}{SH*}{SH*}{SH*}{SH*
}{SH*}{SH*}{SH*}{SHK} {CM5}  {CM+}{CM+}{
CM+}    {SH } {SHN}{SH*}{SH*}{CM+}{CM+}{
CM+}
22 PRINT" {CM2}       {SHU}{SH*}{SH*}{SH*
}{SH*}{SH*}{SH*}{SH*}{SH*}{SH*}{SH*}{SH*
}{SH*}{SH*}{SH*}{SH*}{SHI}{CM5}{CM+}
 {SHN}    {CM+}{CM+}{CM+}
23 PRINT" {CM2}      {SHU}
{SHI} {CM5}{CM+}      {SHN}      {CM+}{CM+}{
```

```
CM+}
24 PRINT" {CM2}     {SHU}                    {
SHI} {SHN}{CM5}{CM+}    {SHN}      {CM+}{C
M+}{CM+}
25 PRINT" {CM2}    {SHU}{SH*}{SH*}{SH*}{S
H*}{SH*}{SH*}{SH*}{SH*}{SH*}{SH*}{SH*}{S
H*}{SH*}{SH*}{SH*}{SHI} {SHN} {CM5}{CM+}
  {SHN}{SH*}{SH*}{SH*}{SH*}{SH*}{SHN}{CM
+}{CM+}{CM+}
26 PRINT" {CM2}    {SHO}                   {S
HP}{SHN}   {CM5}{CM+} {SHN}       {SHN} {CM
+}{CM+}{CM+}
27 PRINT" {CM2}    {SHO}{CMY}{CMY}{CMY}{C
MY}{CMY}{CMY}{CMY}{RVS}{YEL} {OFF}{CM2}{
CMY}{CMY}{CMY}{CMY}{CMY}{CMY}{CMY}{SHP}
  {CMH}{CM5}{SHN}       {SHN}
28 PRINT"{CM2}      {CMH}           {RVS}{YEL}
{SHZ}{OFF}{CM2}         {CMM}    {CMH}
29 PRINT"{CM2}      {CMH}                   {C
MM}  {SHN}
30 PRINT"{CM2}      {CMH}                   {C
MM} {SHN}
31 PRINT"{CM2}     {SHL}{CMP}{CMP}{CMP}{C
MP}{CMP}{CMP}{CMP}{CMP}{CMP}{CMP}{CMP}{C
MP}{CMP}{CMP}{CMP}{SH@}{SHN}
32 PRINT"{ DN}              {CM8}FROM THE {W
HT}ABACUS {CM8}BOOK{ DN}"
33 PRINT"     'ADVENTURE GAMEWRITER'S HAN
DBOOK'"
99 FOR I=1 TO 10000:NEXT
100 REM ------------------------- CHAR
ACTERISTICS
101 :
110 NS=6
120 AO=18
130 AV=6
140 WL=3 :REM WORD LENGTH
150 PL=1
190 DIM SP$[NS],PA[NS,6],OB$[AO],RN$[AO]
,OB[AO]
199 :
200 REM---------- VERBS
201 DATA EXAMINE
202 DATA TAKE
203 DATA DROP
204 DATA OPEN
205 DATA USE
206 DATA BREAK
209 :
```

```
300 REM
301 DATA "LOTS OF BIG TREES", "TRE",1
302 DATA "LOTS OF BIG TREES", "TRE",2
303 DATA "SEVERAL PIECES OF ROCK","ROC",
2
304 DATA "AN OLD WOODEN HUT","HUT",3
305 DATA "A DIRTY JAR","JAR",0
306 DATA "HONEY","HON",0
307 DATA "A WOODEN BOX","BOX",3
308 DATA "A SHELF","SHE",0
309 DATA "SOME EXPLOSIVES","EXP",0
310 DATA"A HOLE IN THE GROUND","HOL",0
311 DATA "A RUSTY IRON CHEST","CHE",0
312 DATA "*SILVER COINS*","SIL",0
313 DATA "A CAVE","CAV",5
314 DATA "A FEROCIOUS LOOKING BEAR", "BEA
",0
315 DATA "LOTS OF SMALL BUSHES","BUS",4
316 DATA "SEVERAL IRON BARS","BAR",6
317 DATA "*NUGGETS*","NUG",5
318 DATA "AN IRON BAR",BAR,0
499 :
500 REM-------------SPACE DESCRIPTIONS
501 DATA "IN THE WOODS",0,0,0,2,0,0
502 DATA "IN THE WOODS",0,0,1,3,0,0
503 DATA "IN THE WOODS BY A ROCKY SLOPE"
,0,4,2,0,0,0
504 DATA "IN A CLEARING IN THE WOODS",3,
0,5,0,0,0
505 DATA "IN A CLEARING BY A MOUNTAIN SL
OPE",0,0,6,4,0,0
506 DATA" AT THE ENTRANCE TUNNEL TO AN O
LD MINE",0,0,0,5,0,0
599 :
600 REM ------ INFORMATION
601 MS$(1)="I CANNOT SEE ANYTHING IN PAR
TICULAR"
602 MS$(2)="I AM NOT THAT STRONG"
603 MS$(3)="WHAT DO YOU MEAN"
604 MS$(4)="THE BEAR TAKES THE HONEY AND
"
605 MS$(5)="DISAPPEARS INTO THE DEPTHS O
F THE CAVE"
698 :
699 REM    TITLE PAGE
700 PRINT"{CLR}":POKE53280,0:POKE53281,0
:PRINT"{WHT}";CHR$(14)
710 PRINT"WELCOME TO THE MINI VERSION OF
"
```

```
715 PRINTSPC(14)"{SHG}{SHO}{SHL}{SHD}{SH
R}{SHU}{SHS}{SHH}     "
720 PRINT"-------------------------------
---------"
725 PRINT"SOME DAYS AGO, WHILE LOOKING F
OR A"
730 PRINT"FORTUNE IN A NEW WORLD, YOU ME
T A"
735 PRINT"CRITICALLY ILL OLD MAN TO WHOM
 YOU GAVE"
740 PRINT"HELP IN HIS LAST HOURS. OUT OF
 GRATITUDE"
745 PRINT"HE TOLD YOU OF HIS GOLD MINE A
ND THE"
750 PRINT"REST OF HIS WEALTH HIDDEN THER
E. MANY "
755 PRINT"DANGERS FACED YOU ON THE WAY T
HERE, SOON"
760 PRINT"YOU WILL HAVE REACHED YOUR GOA
L AND IT"
765 PRINT"WILL BE SEEN WHETHER THE OLD M
AN WAS"
770 PRINT"SPEAKING THE TRUTH OR TALKING
IN A "
775 PRINT"DELIRIUM."
780 :
785 :
790 PRINT"-------------------------------
---------"
799 :
810 FOR I=1TOAV
815 READ VERB$(I):VERB$(I)=LEFT$(VERB$(I
),3)
820 NEXTI
830 FOR OB=1 TO AO
835 READ OB$(OB),RN$(OB),OB(OB)
840 NEXT
845 FOR SPACE = 1 TO NS
850 READ SPACE$(SPACE):
855 FOR DI=1 TO 6:REM DIRECTIONS
860 READ PA(SP,DI)
865 NEXT DI
870 NEXT SPACE
875 :
880 PRINT"DO YOU WANT ADVICE ON WHAT TO
DO NEXT";
885 INPUTEN$
890 IFEN$="Y"THENGOSUB900
895 GOTO1000
```

```
899 :
900 REM   INSTRUCTIONS
910 PRINT"{CLR}";CHR$[14]
920 PRINT"C-64 ADVENTURE SYSTEM VERSION
1.0"
930 PRINT"[C] 1984 BY WALKOWIAK"
940 PRINT"---------------------------
---------"
950 PRINT"IMAGINE A ROBOT THAT YOU CAN C
ONTROL"
951 PRINT"WITH LOTS OF COMMANDS. I AM TH
IS ROBOT"
952 PRINT"AND ON YOUR BEHALF SHALL EXPOS
E MYSELF"
953 PRINT"TO THE DANGERS OF THE BOLDEST
OF ADVENTURES."
954 PRINT"TO ENABLE YOU TO MAKE ME ACT S
ENSIBLY,"
955 PRINT"I SHALL ACCURATELY DESCRIBE TH
E"
956 PRINT"SITUATION IN WHICH I HAPPEN TO
 FIND"
957 PRINT"MYSELF AT ANY GIVEN TIME. WHEN
 YOU TELL"
958 PRINT"ME IN TWO WORDS SUCH AS, TAKE
BAR"
959 PRINT"OR EXAMINE BOX"
960 :
961 PRINT"I UNDERSTAND THE COMMANDS:"
962 PRINT"INVENTORY AND INSTRUCTIONS"
975 PRINT"---------------------------
---------"
980 PRINT"{ DN}{ DN}"SPC[11]"PRESS A KEY
"
985 GETEN$:IFEN$=""THEN985
990 PRINT"{CLR}":PRINTCHR$[142]:RETURN
995 :
999 REM
1000 PRINT"{CLR}":PRINTCHR$[142]
1010 BLANK$="
                 "
1020 DATA NORTH, SOUTH, WEST, EAST, UP,
DOWN
1030 FOR DIR=1 TO 6
1040 READ DIR$[DIR]
1050 NEXT DIR
1070 PRINT"{CLR}":POKE53280,0:POKE53281,
0:PRINT" "
1080 PRINT"{BLU}"
```

```
1090 POKE211,0:POKE214,0:SYS58732
1100 FOR LINE=1TO10
1110 PRINTBLANK$
1120 NEXT LINE
1130 POKE214,0:POKE211,0:SYS58732
1140 PRINT"I AM ";
1150 PRINT SPACES$[PLAYER]
1160 PRINT"I SEE ";
1170 FOR I=1 TO AO
1180 IF OB[I]<>PLAYER THEN 1210
1190 IF POS[O]+LEN[OB$[I]]+2<=39 THENPRI
NTOB$[I];", ";:GOTO1210
1200 IF POS[O]+LEN[OB$[I]]+2> 39 THENPRI
NT:GOTO1190
1210 NEXT I
1220 PRINTCHR$[157];CHR$[157];"."
1230 PRINTBLANK$
1240 PRINT"I MAY PROCEED ";
1250 FOR DIR=1 TO 6
1260 IF PA[PL,DI]=OTHEN1310
1270 IF POS[O]=14 THEN PRINT DIR$[DIR];:
GOTO1310
1280 IF POS[O]+LEN[DI$[DIR]]<37 THEN PRI
NT", ";DIR$[DIR];:GOTO1310
1290 IF POS[O]+LEN[DI$[DIR]]>=37 THEN PR
INT", ":PRINT DIR$[DIR];:GOTO1310
1300 IF POS[O]<16 AND POS[O]>2 THEN PRIN
T", ";DIR$[DIR];:GOTO1310
1310 NEXT DIR
1320 PRINT"."
1330 PRINT"----------------------------
----------"
1340 IF OB[12]=-1 AND OB[17]=-1 THEN GOT
O 4800
1390 POKE211,0:POKE214,24:SYS58732:PRINT
"{WHT}";:INPUT"WHAT SHALL I DO";EN$:PRIN
T"{BLU}"
1400 IF LEN[EN$]>2 THEN 1500
1410 IF EN$="N" AND PASSAGE[PLA,1]<>0 TH
EN PLA=PASSAGE[PLA,1]:PRINT"O.K.":GOTO10
80
1420 IF EN$="S" AND PASSAGE[PLA,2]<>0 TH
EN PLA=PASSAGE[PLA,2]:PRINT"O.K.":GOTO10
80
1430 IF EN$="W" AND PASSAGE[PLA,3]<>0 TH
EN PLA=PASSAGE[PLA,3]:PRINT"O.K.":GOTO10
80
1440 IF EN$="E" AND PASSAGE[PLA,4]<>0 TH
EN PLA=PASSAGE[PLA,4]:PRINT"O.K.":GOTO10
```

```
80
1450 IF EN$="U" AND PASSAGE[PLA,5]<>0 TH
EN PLA=PASSAGE[PLA,5]:PRINT"O.K.":GOTO10
80
1460 IF EN$="D" AND PASSAGE[PLA,6]<>0 TH
EN PLA=PASSAGE[PLA,6]:PRINT"O.K.":GOTO10
80
1470 IF LEN[ENTRY$]<3THEN      PRINT"YOU
CAN'T GO THAT WAY":GOTO1080
1490 IF LEN[ENTRY$]>6 THEN GOTO 2000
1498 :
1499 REM -------- START OF INVENTORY
1500 IF LEFT$[ENTRY$,3]<>"INV"THEN GOTO
1900
1510 PRINT"I AM CARRYING THE FOLLOWING
WITH ME:"
1520 FOR I=1 TO AO
1530 IF OB[I]=-1THEN PRINT OB$[I]
1540 NEXT I
1550 GOTO 1080
1560 REM -------- END OF INVENTORY
1561 :
1899 REM     INSTRUCTIONS
1900 IF LEFT$[EN$,3]<>"INS"THEN1950
1910 GOSUB900
1920 GOTO1080
1950 IFLEFT$[EN$,3]<>"END"THEN2000
1960 PRINT"(CLR)THE AUTHOR WISHES YOU MO
RE SUCCESS NEXT TIME" :END
1990 :
2000 LN=LEN[ENTRY$]
2010 FOR EL=1TOLN
2020 TEST$=MID$[ENTRY$,EL,1]
2030 IF TEST$<> " "THEN NEXT EL
2040 EV$=LEFT$[ENTRY$,3]
2050 RL=LN-EL
2060 IF RL<0 THEN 2090
2070 EO$=RIGHT$[ENTRY$,RL]
2080 EO$=LEFT$[EO$,WL]
2090 FOR VN=1 TO AV
2100 IF EV$=VERB$[VN] THEN 2130
2110 NEXT VN
2120 PRINT"I DO NOT UNDERSTAND THAT VERB
!":GOTO1080
2130 FOR N=1 TO AO
2140 IF EO$=RN$[N] THEN 2200
2150 NEXT N
2160 PRINT"I DO NOT KNOW THIS OBJECT!":G
OTO1080
```

```
2169 :
2170 REM
2200 ON VN GOTO 5000,6000,7000,8000,9000
,10000
2201 :
4498 :
4499 :
4500 PRINTCHR$[147]: REM PLAYER DEAD
4600 PRINT"THIS IS THE END!":PRINTMS$[0]
4610 PRINT"{ DN}{ DN} I AM DEAD":PRINT
4620 INPUT"SHALL I TRY AGAIN";A$
4630 IF LEFT$[A$,1]="Y"THEN RUN
4640 PRINT"CHR$[147]:END
4641 :
4799 :
4800 PRINT"{CLR}"
4810 PRINT"WELL DONE"
4820 PRINT
4830 PRINT"YOU SOLVED THE ADVENTURE"
4840 PRINT
4899 END
4998 :
4999 REM
5000 IF OB[N]<>PL AND OB[N]<>-1 THEN GOT
O 5900
5002 IF N=1 THEN PRINT MS$[1]:GOTO1080
5003 IF N=3 THEN PRINT MS$[1]:GOTO1080
5004 IF N=4 THENPRINT"IN A CORNER THERE
IS A SHELF.":OB[8]=PL:GOTO1080
5005 IFN=5THENPRINT"THE JAR IS FULL OF H
ONEY.":GOTO1080
5006 IFN=6THENPRINTMS$[1]:GOTO1080
5007 IFN=7ANDOB[9]=0THENPRINT"IN THE BOX
 IS SOME EXPLOSIVE.":GOTO1080
5008 IF N=8 AND OB[5]=0 THEN PRINT"ON TH
E SHELF THERE IS A JAR":OB[5]=PL:GOTO108
0
5009 IF N=8 AND OB[5]<>0 THENPRINTMS$[1]
:GOTO1080
5010 IFN=10THENPRINT"IN THE HOLE IS AN I
RON CHEST":OB[11]=PL:GOTO1080
5011 IF N=11ANDNOTFL[1]THENPRINT"IT IS S
ECURED WITH AN IRON CHAIB":GOTO1080
5012 IFN=11ANDFL[1]ANDNOTFL[2]THENPRINT"
I CAN'T SEE ANYTHING FROM THE OUTSIDE":G
OTO1080
5013 IFN=11ANDFL[1]ANDFL[2]THENPRINT"IT
IS FULL OF SILVER COINS":OB[12]=PL :GOTO
1080
```

```
5014 IFN=12THENPRINT"THATS JUST WHAT I'M
 LOOKING FOR!":GOTO1080
5015 IFN=13THENPRINT"I'VE WOKE A BEAR UP
 ":OB[14]=PL:GOTO1080
5017 IFN=15THENPRINT"THERES A HOLE IN GR
OUND":OB[10]=PL:GOTO1080
5018 IFN=16THENPRINT"THEY LOOK VERY STRO
NG":GOTO1080
5019 IFN=17THENPRINT"THIS IS REAL GOLD !
"GOTO1080
5900 REM OBJECT NOT PRESENT
5901 IF N=1 AND PL=2 THEN PRINT"MS$[1]:G
OTO1080
5902 IFN=6ANDOB[5]=-1THEN PRINT"IT IS SW
EET AND GOOD":GOTO1080
5903 IFN=6ANDOB[5]<>-1THENPRINT"I HAVEN'
T SEEN ANY HONEY":GOTO1080
5904 IFN=9ANDOB[7]=PLOROB[7]=-1 THEN PRI
NT"IT LOOKS VERY EXPLOSIVE!":GOTO1080
5905 IFM=9THENPRINT"THE EXPLOSIVE LOOKS
DANGEROUS!":GOTO1080
5910 IF N=1ANDPL=5ANDOB[14]=5THENPRINT"I
 SEEM TO WHET HIS APPETITE!":GOTO1080
5990 PRINT"I DO NOT SEE ANYTHING LIKE TH
AT HERE!":GOTO1080
6000 IF OB[N]<>PLAND OB[N]<>-1 THEN GOTO
 6900
6001 IF N=1 THEN PRINTMS$[2]:GOTO1080
6002 IFN=3THENPRINTMS$[2]:GOTO1080
6003 IFN=4THENPRINTMS$[3]:GOTO1080
6004 IFN=8THENPRINTMS$[2]:GOTO1080
6005 IF N=11 THEN PRINTMS$[2]:GOTO1080
6006 IFN=10THENPRINTMS$[3]:GOTO1080
6007 IFN=13THENPRINTMS$[3]:GOTO1080
6008 IFN=15THENPRINTMS$[2]:GOTO1080
6010 IF N=5 THEN OB[5]=-1:PRINT"O.K.":GO
TO1080
6011 IFN=6THENOB[5]=-1:PRINT"OK":GOTO108
0
6012 IFN=7THENOB[7]=-1:PRINT"OK":GOTO108
0
6014 IFN=12THENPRINT"OK":OB[12]=-1:GOTO1
080
6015 IF N=1ANDPL=5THEN MS$[0]="THE BEAR
HAS KILLED ME.":GOTO4500
6016 IFN=16THENPRINT"OK":OB[18]=-1:GOTO1
080
6017 IFN=17ANDFL[3]THENPRINT"OK":OB[17]=
-1:GOTO1080
```

```
6018 IF N=17ANDNOTPL[3]THEN MS$[0]="THE
BEAR IS ATTACKING ME.":GOTO4500
6900 IF N=9 THEN MS$[0]="IT EXPLODED WHE
N I TOUCHED IT.":GOTO4500
7000 REM
7005 IF OB[N]<>-1 THEN PRINT"BUT I DON'T
 HAVE ANYTHING LIKE THAT.":GOTO1080
7010 IFN=6ANDPL=5THENOB[6]=0:FL[3]=-1:PR
INTMS$[4]:PRINTMS$[5]:OB[14]=0:GOTO
7020 IFN=5ANDPL=5THENOB[5]=0:FL[3]=-1:PR
INTMS$[4]:PRINTMS$[5]:OB[14]=0:GOTO1080
7900 OB[N]=PL:PRINT"O.K.":GOTO1080
8000 IF OB[N]<>PL AND OB[N]<>-1 THEN PRI
NT"THERE IS NOTHING LIKE THAT HERE.":GOT
O1080
8005 IFN=4ANDPL=3THENPRINT"THE HUT WAS O
PEN":GOTO1080
8010 IF N=5THEN PRINT"O.K.":GOTO1080
8020 IFN=11ANDNOTFL[1]THENPRINT"THE CHAI
N STOPS YOU DOING THAT":GOTO1080
8025 IFN=11ANDFL[1]THEN PRINT"O.K. - THE
 LID FOLDS BACKWARDS.":FL[2]=-1:GOTO1080
8999 PRINT"I DO NOT UNDERSTAND WHAT YOU
MEAN":GOTO1080
9000 REMVERB=USE
9010 IFN=16ANDPL=4THENPRINT"THE CHAIN BR
EAKS.":FL[1]=-1: GOTO1080
9999 PRINT"I DON'T UNDERSTAND WHAT YOU M
EAN.":GOTO1080
10000 IFN=18ANDPL=4THENOB[18]=-1:PRINT"T
HE CHAIN BREAKS.":FL[1]=-1:GOTO1080
10010 IFN=18ANDPL=4ANDOB[18]<>-1THENPRIN
T"WHAT WITH?":GOTO1080
10999 PRINT"I DON'T UNDERSTAND WHAT YOU
MEAN.":GOTO1080

READY.
```

'ADVENTURE GAMEWRITER'S HANDBOOK'

```
1 REM   -- GOLDRUSH, VERSION 1.0 --
2 REM      [C] 1984 BY WALKOWIAK
10 REM -------------------- TITLE PIC
TURE
11 POKE53281,11:POKE53280,12:PRINTCHR$[1
42]
12 PRINT""
13 PRINT"
14 PRINT"
15 PRINT"
16 PRINT"
17 PRINT"
18 PRINT"   I    [C] 1984     I
19 PRINT"   I       BY         I
20 PRINT"   IJOERG WALKOWIAK I
21 PRINT"
22 PRINT"
23 PRINT"
24 PRINT"
25 PRINT"
26 PRINT"
27 PRINT"
28 PRINT"
29 PRINT"
30 PRINT"
31 PRINT"
32 PRINT"          from the abacus book"
```

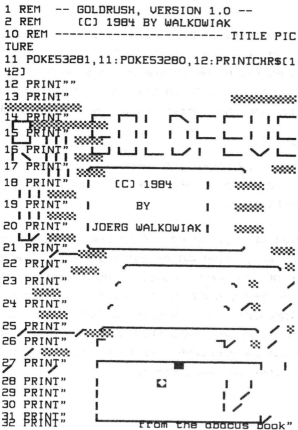

4. FROM THE GOOD TO THE PERFECT ADVENTURE

If you have played with the miniversion of GOLD FEVER or
have created an adventure yourself using the techniques
developed so far, you will agree with me that popular
programs of the adventure type have already reached a very
high standard.

Even so, from time to time we find adventure games offering
further extras. To beat the competition, either the user
friendliness has been increased or use has been made of the
trivialities of everyday life in the realization of the
game, trivialities that only make the player's life more
difficult.

On top of this there are already a number of programs that
draw attention to unique features, this involving
expenditure on advertising.

The player is also offered sound, from single beeps and
cheeps, signaling an understood or non executable command,
to the imitation of the human voice. Unfortunately the
value of all this from the point of view of the game is
precisely nil. Therefore one should think twice about
sacrificing one's money on cheap showmanship and consider
whether it would not be preferable to have your adventure
worlds expanded by your own programming.

4.1 USER FRIENDLINESS

This is always being demanded in the case of business
programs, so why not in the case of game?

There are adventures that do not even tell the player by
what routes he can get away from a dangerous place. They
drive him to despair with the statement "You can't go in
that direction" following input of all points of the
compass.

It's a good thing, sometimes, if the player has to tear his
hair out, but it does seem to me that these programs have
been written in order to say "We guarantee that you will
need months to get to know all the places in this
adventure!"

Fortunately this criticism cannot apply to our adventure
system. Nevertheless the absence of any possibility of
storing the state of the game at any given moment means that
the player will quickly lose all pleasure in the game.

Unfortunately this applies especially to adventures to whose
development we have devoted a great deal of energy and of
whose complexity and intelligently set traps we may be
particularly proud.

Let us help the player, who in any case must have more than
seven lives, to get to know all the possible ways of dying
in adventures and let us create the technical prerequisites
to enable him, richer by many experiences, to continue the
game from this point on. Then, if he does not make timely
use of this option, he can only blame himself.

4.2 SAVE GAME/LOAD GAME

Let us first consider how a certain scene in the game differs from the starting position.

The first thing we notice is the player, who has been moving about more or less determinedly. Then we think of the objects that he has taken, discarded, destroyed, used, or eaten, of objects that no longer exist, and of things that have appeared in the game for the first time.

Apart from these visible and perhaps less important contents of variables, less important because they can be checked, we must save the changes made to control the course of the game, otherwise it can happen that despite all the necessary objects being present an action does not bring the desired success.

Let us think about flags that cannot always be used for checking the course of a connected question, but can be used for checking seemingly unconnected events.

The same applies to our direction table. As we shall see later, extensive changes are quite common here.

Briefly put, the contents of the variables PL,OB[], FL[], and PA[] must be stored on the disk or cassette as a sequential file before a game is ended.

4.2.1 External data storage

In addition to the internal data storage, in which the data
is filed in the actual working storage of the CPU and   are
permanently at   its   disposal,   external   storage   is also
necessary for dealing with data of any kind.   Such storage
extend the storage of a computer in almost any way   required
and   in essence serve to document and prepare large   amounts
of   data.   Representative of this kind of   equipment are
punched   cards and tapes, magnetic tapes, disk and   platen
drives, and our 1541 floppy disk or Cassette data set.

Apart from different capacities and access times,   there are
also differences in the method of data storage.

Storage devices such as a tape punch/reader or the data   set
use   what   are called files and can best be compared   to   an
ancient   parchment   scroll,   while   a disk or   platen   drive
generally uses relative files.

Both   methods   have   their   advantages   and   disadvantages,
particularly   in respect to the space required and the   time
needed to file a specific data record.

Thus each address in a customer file will need a card of its
own,   while   on the scroll all addresses will be entered   as
close   as possible together to save paper.   If however   you
are   looking for the address of customer 234,   you take   the
234th card,   since they are of course all numbered.   In the
case   of the scroll it will not be possible to avoid reading
all   addresses   or at least counting them through   from   the
beginning.

Readers who would now like to deal more with files should
review this with the appropriate literature, otherwise it
may be enough to say that sequential storage is just the
right process for our problem, since we want to store the
contents of our variables one after the other and later
reload them, that is to say we do not need special access
methods.

4.2.2 SAVE GAME

It will be expedient to transfer the data within loops whose
structure we base on the initialization part of our
adventure. For this purpose however it will be necessary to
extend the characteristics of the program by the number of
flags used, since this must also be saved.

It will be necessary to alter program line 1500 in order to
build the new routines into the interrogation of the special
commands:

```
160   AF=3
1500 IF LEFT$[ENTRY$,3]<> "INV" THEN GOTO 1600
```

If the player's last input is not the command Inventory, a
number of jumps are executed and an identity with one of the
brief commands is established:

```
1599 REM --------------------- SAVE GAME
1600 IF LEFT$[ENTRY$,4]  =   "SAVE" THEN GOTO 1700
1699 REM --------------------- LOAD GAME
1700 IF LEFT$[ENTRY$,4]  =   "LOAD" THEN GOTO 1900
```

Before the operating system of our C-64 can transfer the data, it must first be given some information as direction of transfer, path of transport, and addresses, a task done by the open command.

    1620 OPEN 2,8,2,"@0:GAME,S,W"

After execution of this line a data file called "GAME" is available on the disk in the drive with the device number 8. This data file can be described as a sequential file [S] [W =Write]. The @ character is necessary in order to be able to store an advanced game under the same name.

Users of the data set input the following line instead:

    1620 OPEN 1,1,1,"GAME"

and change every #2 to #1.

After this preparation nothing stands in the way of transferring our playing data. The output of the data to the disk is executed in a similar way to an output onto the screen.

The PRINT# command is used to redirected the output to the correct file.

A concluding close command protects us from subsequent errors before we return to the main program.

```
1630  FOR I = 1 TO AO
1631  PRINT#2,OB[I]
1632  NEXT I
1635  FOR SPACES = 1 TO NS
1636  FOR D1 = 1 TO 6
1637  PRINT#2, PA[SP,DI]
1638  NEXT DI
1639  NEXT SP
1645  FOR I = 1 TO AF
1646  PRINT#2, FL[I]
1647  NEXT I
1650  CLOSE 2
1670  PRINT CHR$ [147]:GOTO 1080
```

To reconstruct a given situation, it is essential to transfer this data back to the corresponding variables, a task taken over by an almost identical program part:

```
1720  OPEN 2,8,2,"GAME,S,R,"
1725  INPUT#2, PL
1730  FOR I = 1 TO AO
1731  INPUT#1, OB[I]
1732  NEXT
1735  FOR SP = 1 TO NS
1736  FOR DI - 1 TO 6
1737  INPUT#2, PA[SP,DI]
1738  NEXT DI
1739  NEXT SPACE
1745  FOR I = 1 TO AF
1746  INPUT#2, FL[I]
1747  NEXT I
1750  CLOSE 2
1770  PRINT CHR$[147] : GOTO 1080
```

When using the data set, use the following line:

    1720 OPEN 1,1,0, "GAME"

Naturally you must again change all #2's to #1's.

This would solve the task so far as cassette systems are connected, but disk users should avail themselves of the possibilities offered by disks and, before continuing the game, satisfy themselves that the operation went perfectly.

Perhaps, when the Save function is called up, the program disk, which for safety reasons has a write protect on it, is still in the drive or the disk concerned is full - there are many things that could result in making all the previous work a waste of time.

Page 36 of the disk operating manual tells how the error channel is read. Our job now is to evaluate the information thus obtained and, if necessary, pass it on to the player.

Therefore let us add the following lines to our program:

```
1679   REM -------------------- DISK ERROR
1680   OPEN 1,8,15
1681   INPUT#1,A,B$,C,D
1682   IFA <> OTHENPRINT: PRINT "ERROR:";:
       PRINTA,B$C,D:FORI=1TO5000:NEXT:CLOSE2:CLOSE1:GOTO
       1080
1683   CLOSE1
1684   RETURN : REM ---- END OF ERROR -----
```

and call it at the necessary points:

```
1660   GOSUB 1680
1760   GOSUB 1680
```

To equip our program even more luxuriously, we shall add a
few more lines.   It is not at all necessary for us to
restrict ourselves to only one file for storage.   A second
file will even be essential if other members of our current
family start liking adventures and want to try their hand at
the same game.

Therefore   let us give the players a free choice and allow
them to choose among all conceivable names up to the maximum
length of sixteen letters.

Let us also add a few more print and control   commands to
ensure that the clean display of the screen image is
maintained.

A subroutine completed in this way will then look like the
listing printed on the following pages.

```
1599 REM ---------------------------- SAVE GAME
1600 IF LEFT$(EI$,4)<>"SAVE" THEN GOTO 1700
1605 PRINT" "SPC(10);:INPUT" ENTER NAME";EN$
1610 IF LEN(EN$)>16 THEN 1605
1615 PRINT" SAVING ";EN$
1620 OPEN 2,8,2"@0:"+EN$+",S,W"
1625 PRINT#2,PL
1627 PRINT#2, WE:PRINT#2,LM:PRINT#2,LW
1628 PRINT#2, ZU
1630 FOR I=1 TO AO
1631 PRINT#2,OB(I)
1632 NEXT I
1633 PRINT".";
1635 FOR SP=1 TO NS
1636 FOR DI=1 TO 6
1637 PRINT#2, PA(SP,DI)
1638 NEXT DI
1639 NEXT SP
1640 PRINT".";
1645 FOR I=1 TO AF
1646 PRINT#2,FL(I)
1647 NEXT I
1648 PRINT".";
1650 CLOSE 2
1660 GOSUB 1680
1670 PRINT"(clr)":GOTO 1080
1678 :
1679 REM --------------------DISK ERROR
1680 OPEN1,8,15
1681 INPUT#1,A,B$,C,D
1682 IFA<>OTHENPRINT":PRINT"ERROR:
     ":PRINTB$:FORI=1TO 5000:NEXT:CLOSE2
1683 CLOSE1
```

```
1684 RETURN : REM ----------- END
1698 :
1699 REM ---------------------- LOAD GAME
1700 IF LEFT$(EN$,4)<>"LOAD" THEN GOTO 1800
1705  PRINT" "SPC(10)"LOAD GAME":INPUT"    WHAT    IS
THE GAME'S NAME";EN$
1710 IF LEN(EN$)>16 THEN 1805
1715 PRINT"  LOADING "EN$"";
1720 OPEN 2,8,2,EN$+",S,R"
1725 INPUT#2,PL
1726 PRINT".";
1727 INPUT#2, WE:INPUT#2,L1:INPUT#2,LM:INPUT#2,LW
1728 INPUT#2, ZU
1730 FOR I=1 TO AO
1731 INPUT#2,OB(I)
1732 NEXT I
1733 PRINT".";
1735 FOR SP=1 TO NS
1736 FOR DI=1 TO 6
1737 INPUT#2, PA(SP,DI)
1738 NEXT DI
1739 NEXT SP
1740 PRINT".";
1745 FOR I = 1 TO AF
1746 INPUT#2,FL(I)
1747 NEXT I
1748 PRINT".";
1750 CLOSE 2
1760 GOSUB 1680
1770 PRINT"{clr}":GOTO 1080
1771 REM ----------------- END OF GAME
```

4.3 THE VOCABULARY

Frequently the correct choice of words makes an adventure game a torment, since, as a player, one is compelled to use the same mode of expression as the programmer, which is not always easy.

"Take knife" is not so bad, but the knife will have a job to do. A knife is a welcome object, since outputs such as "Throw knife away", "Grind knife", or "Sharpen knife" do not call for all that much imagination and likewise can be clearly interpreted.

When the knife has fulfilled its function, one will sooner or later want to get rid of it. In some games this can be done by deliberately losing it. "Drop knife" is somewhat more effective than "Lose knife", but automatically the question of where occurs. up. This input, it is true, contradicts the usual rules of the game, but nevertheless should be tried, at least on our system.

Let us finally reconsider an example given in the first few pages of this book. How do we get into the crown of the tree? Perhaps with "Climb tree"? All we get again is the message that the word "climb" has not been understood, so do we give up or go on brooding? It will not be possible to avoid trying verbs such as "up" or "mount", and if the action is really essential, a successful result will sooner or later be achieved.

Naturally problems of this kind are not very nice, and as this chapter deals with the question of perfecting our adventure system, we shall look for suitable solutions.

4.3.1 SYNONYMS

As a first suggestion, one way of solving the language problem would be to incorporate synonymous words in sufficient numbers. As the example of the tree shows, however, the logical provision of synonymous words can greatly increase the size of a program. This means an immense amount of additional routine work and severely restricts the free memory, which is becoming smaller and smaller.

Nevertheless, again taking Gold Fever as an example, let us suggest a solution, one that is almost convincing on account of its brevity and simplicity. Needless to say, it is not a question of essential program lines. It is up to you to decide whether you are prepared to be content with the subsequent suggestion aimed at improving the user friendliness.

A person playing Gold Fever will in space 3 have his first chance of not finding the right word immediately when he attempts to take a closer look at the wooden hut. So far he will have failed with "Examine wooden hut". He will succeed only with "Examine hut".

If the second idea is to be understood at all, we must first expand our vocabulary:

```
120 A0=9
319 DATA "-", "WOODEN HUT",0
```

We can spare ourselves a detailed description. Likewise the
zero representing the location becomes obligatory.   Finally
no further hut must appear either in the inventory or in a
space.

All that is needed is the reference name to enable the
adventure driver to ascertain the corresponding object
number, which is done on line 2140.

Normally the execution of the program is continued in line
2200 with a jump to the respective command execution.   Here
naturally there is not a single condition that would be
fulfilled, since nowhere is a value of 19 demanded for N.
To avoid having to add to these lines, we insert the
following dodge:

```
2140 IF EO$=RN$[N] THEN 2165
2164 REM ----------------------SYNONYMS
2165 IF N=19 THEN N=4
```

Now exactly the same actions are carried out with the wooden
hut as with the hut.

Enabling our program to understand a multiplicity of verbs
involves even less work.

A word introducing the same action is likewise placed at the
disposal of the adventure vocabulary, and the jump table is
simply supplemented by the jump target already once used.

In this way we extend Gold Fever with the function "LOOK
AT", making it identical with "EXAMINE":

```
130    AV=7
207    DATA LOOK AT
2200   ON VN GOTO 5000,6000,7000,8000,9000,
       10000,5000
```

As you see, our system can very easily be extended by synonymous verbs, so we should not give up this bonus.

We do not need to pay much attention to synonyms of the objects, since in any case they are not of the same importance, the heading lines to the game nearly always giving enough clues, except in the case of graphics adventures.

We can however make things even easier for the player, so that he can really concentrate on solving the problems and does not become lost in his search for the right words.

What if an adventure exposed its entire vocabulary on request and produced a list of all existing objects and possible verbs?

A picture such as the one on the next page should eliminate all problems of word selection, and the player does not lose time or interest with senseless inputs.

VOCABULARY

I UNDERSTAND THE FOLLOWING VERBS

EXAMINE

TAKE

DROP

OPEN

USE

DESTROY

LIGHT

FILL

ENTER

EXTINQUISH

FIX

PRESS A KEY

Let us imagine a player who is not yet familiar with Gold
Fever. Without having played very much, he will, if he can
think more or less consistently and logically, immediately
develop a strategy that will quickly bring him to his goal
in the solution of the problems.

He immediately knows the entire vocabulary and knows that
somewhere there is a jar, that somewhere there is a chest,
and will at once develop a strong yearning for silver and
gold nuggets. Then he will consider what objects can be
destroyed and his choice will fall on the jar, the hut, and
the chain.

He endeavors to find the treasure chest, and after realizing
that an iron chain is stopping him from inspecting the

contents, he tries to destroy it, but he can hardly do so with his bare hands. A further VOC will then give him the idea that the iron bar is presumably the only object suitable for this job.

But also the tension caused by the dangers is relived as it does not escape the player's notice that the world is inhabited by not only himself but also by a bear!

Accordingly another of the programmer's tasks will be to decide carefully whether he wants to expose the entire vocabulary used in the adventure or only part of it.

This could be done without any problem by means of a further screen outputting a number of the more important words, but it would be counterproductive to our aim, which is the development of a universal adventure system, because this screen would have to be revised for each program.

In the case of large adventures with a corresponding large vocabulary, the listing of the vocabulary does however make perfect sense, so we do not propose dispensing with it when developing our adventure system.

For this reason the adventure driver takes over the handling of the VOC command. To ensure a really universal use of this program section, the words to be output must be ascertained from the playing data of the adventure concerned.

It has already been briefly mentioned that the BASIC command RESTORE sets the DATA pointer to the beginning of the data block and that the next READ will again read the first element in the list to a variable.

Fortunately the arrangement of our adventure data fits in well with such a procedure, as first the verbs and then the objects are named. No execution time must be spent on reading the rest of the data.

Let us build in the appropriate subroutine after the INV, SAVE, and LOAD routine:

```
1800 IF LEFT$(ENTRY$,3)<> "VOC" THEN GOTO 1900
1805 PRINT CHR$(147):PRINTCHR$(158);
     "I UNDERSTAND THE FOLLOWING VERBS";CHR$(17);
     CHR$(17)
1806 RESTORE
```

Any subsequent READs now acts like the first READ command. Therefore let us change the corresponding program lines from part 1 with a modification that allows the data being read to no longer be stored, but only printed out on the screen:

```
1810  FOR I=1 TO AV
1820  READ VO$ : PRINT VO$
1830  NEXT I
```

Following this we will give the player enough time to study the list of verbs. The same must be done with the printing out of the objects, so we insert the corresponding lines as a subroutine, this being called with a GOSUB at the points concerned:

```
1840   GOSUB 1890
1845   PRINTCHR$[147]:PRINT
       "AND THE FOLLOWING OBJECTS ARE KNOWN TO ME:"
       CHR$[17]
1850   FOR I=1 TO AO
1860   READ VO$,VO$,X : PRINT VO$
1870   NEXT I
1880   GOSUB 1890:PRINT CHR$[147]: GOTO 1080
1890   PRINTSPC[24];CHR$[17]; "PRESS KEY";
1895   GET ENTRY$: IF ENTRY$=""THEN 1895
1896   PRINT CHR$[147] : RETURN
```

It should be noted that in BASIC, DATA lines are read
sequentially. Therefore line 1860 first allocates the
detailed object description to the string variable VO$.
Because we do not need this long text at this point, the
description is then immediately overwritten with the
reference name.

To conclude the listing of the entire vocabulary, the
subroutine is again called from line 1890, so that, after a
further key has been pressed, the adventure may be
continued.

The above lines will now work as planned, at least so long
as not more than twenty words have to be output. When this
figure is exceeded, the time that the first words are on the
screen will hardly be long enough to be of any help to the
player.

To solve the problem, we introduce the check variable called
LINE. This is set to zero at the start of the output and
raised by one for each output.

117

At twenty words we clear the screen and set the counter back
to one.

```
1849  LINE=0
1850  FOR I=1 TO AO
1855  LINE=LINE+1
1860  READ VO$,VO$,X : PRINT VO$
1865  IF LINE=20 THEN GOSUB 1890
1866  IF LINE=20 THEN LINE=1 : PRINT CHR$(147)
1870  NEXT I
```

Running the program now brings the required result, but the
contractions appearing [EXA,OPE, or whatever] in no way meet
the standard of our programs.

To achieve a more satisfactory result, we change the verbs
and objects in the DATA lines provided for them [200 - 500]
and take the, trouble to write them out, regardless of the
relevant word length.

With this manipulation it now becomes necessary to make a
further addition to lines 815 and 835.   After all, we do
not want to waste the memory area provided for the
variables.

Why must the whole word be stored when for the clear
identification of a move only three or four letters are of
importance?

```
815 READ VERB$(I):VERB$(I)=LEFT$(VERB$(I),WL)
835 READ OB$(OBJECT), OB(OBJECT):
    RN$(OB)=LEFT$(RN$(OB),WL)
```

4.4 HELP

The development of a Help routine is the final step aimed at
increasing the user friendliness of our adventure.

If the player thinks he can move no farther, he will try to
obtain some helpful information merely by inputting HELP.

If it is a simple game, then enough information is given in
the course of it, we can make the matter easy for ourselves:

```
1959 REM --------------------- HELP
1960 IF LEFT$(ENTRY$,4)<> "HELP" THEN GOTO 2000
1970 PRINT"I CAN REPEAT THE RULES OF THE GAME.":
     PRINT "DO YOU WANT THAT?"
1971 GET EN$:IF EN$="" THEN 1971
1972 IF EN$="Y" THENGOSUB 900
1975 GOTO 1080
1979 REM --------------------- END OF HELP
```

A standard answer that is even more frequent is "You should
try everything! - Try examining things!". Usually however,
at least in adventure games of more recent date, advice is
given that sometimes is not of much help, because the player
cannot understand it.

Since it is a one-word command, the help required is not
related to any particular object. In view of the player's
difficulties this does not make an evaluation of the
situation exactly easy.

Finally only the player's location space is available to the
program as a working basis, so it is not surprising that in

problematic spaces many adventures repeatedly output the same message to the player, a message he cannot understand because he has been thinking about another problem.

As a typical example let us take a scene from space 4. The player has discovered the treasure chest and for some time has been struggling in vain with the troublesome iron chain. In this situation the following message would be conceivable:

```
1970  IF  PL=4  THEN  PRINT"A    LEVER   WILL
INCREASE YOUR STRENGTH.":GOTO1080
```

What could a player who in space 4 asks for help do with the suggestion, that he should think a lever when he has not yet found the chest and accordingly cannot have discovered the chain?

If one wants to spoil the player and in particularly difficult situations lead him to the solution step by step, this will not be possible, as the above example shows, without the formulation of extensive tests and condition. Once again the flags and the storage places for all kinds of objects seem predestined to perform this task.

Taking the chest as an example again, let us try out this kind of carefully measured help, which of course is not intended to mean that this scene is to be regarded as particularly difficult:

```
606 MS$[6]="HOW CAN I DESTROY THE CHAIN?"
1970  IF PL=4 AND OB[10]=0 THEN PRINT"I NEARLY FELL
INTO A PIT.":GOTO1080
1971  IF  PL=4  AND  OB[11]=PL AND  NOT  FL[2]  THEN
PRINTMS$[6];:PRINTMS$[7]:GOTO 1080
```

Let us remember that on passing the space concerned only the
bushes are visible at first and that the hole in the ground
still has to be discovered. If however the player is warned
of the possibility of a near fall into a pit, he will
probably pay more attention to this obstacle.

At this point any further attempt with Help will offer no
particular advantage. Only after the chest becomes one of
the things in the space as a visible object is it suggested
to the player that inspection of the contents calls for the
chain to be destroyed and the lid to be opened.

It is hoped that the player will then be able to carry out
these actions by himself. If he cannot, it might be worth
his considering whether it would not be better for him to
read a novel or play arcade action games.

As when programming the other actions, a safety statement
will again form the conclusion to the help command. this
statement is always executed when no specially defined
situation has arisen:

```
1971:
1972:
1975 PRINT"FIRST LOOK,  THEN THINK, AND FINALLY ACT
! ":GOTO 1080
```

4.5 THE PLAYER'S MOTIVATION

Our next suggestion for better adventures will extend our adventure driver by a final one-word command.

For their solution adventure programs do take a certain amount of time, but if one plays them for days on end and sees no progress at all, one asks oneself one day whether one should not load another game.

For this reason I consider adventure games that use a point system that shows the player how far he still is from his final goal considerably more appealing.

It is however necessary to consider on what basis the scoring is to be carried out. For every treasure found or for every task solved in an adventure the usual version provides for a certain number of points. In addition to being told "Of 100 possible points you have 40" the player is also given the percentage, as a result of which the score is more easily and more accurately evaluated. Scott Adam's **"Adventureland"** can again be taken as an example. Thirteen treasures give a bad number of points, but with more than 50 percent the player knows that he has covered half the journey.

An alternative solution will reward each step forward and not deter one by deducting a certain number of points for any help given. Likewise any mistake resulting in death will not make any significant difference, so that in an extreme case even a negative value can not be scored. It is this method that encourages one to make repeated attempts to find a solution, since after all it should be possible to

score more points than the friend who likewise has reached
the goal.

If an adventure is to be equipped in such a manner, the
programmer's job starts with the selection of suitable
sequences.   After all the mere finding of an object is not
meant to be worth any points at this stage.   The player may
however expect a reward if he has tricked some dangerous
monsters or found some secret passages.

Before we now go into the practical execution of various
versions in detail, we first give the driver an
understanding of the command "SCORE":

```
    1500 IF LEFT$(ENTRY$,3)<>"INV" THEN GOTO 1560
    1559 REM -------------------------- SCORE
    1560 IF LEFT$(ENTRY$,3)<>"SCO" THEN GOTO 1600
```

To store the score obtained, we then enter the variable
SCORE. Here it is important to see that this is set to zero
with every fresh start and accordingly also in the event of
death of the main figure.
Naturally the score obtained says nothing unless it is
related to the maximum number of points possible. Hence:

```
    170 WM=20 :REM MAXIMUM POINTS OF THE MINIVERSION
    171 WE=0 :REM 0 POINTS
    1561 PRINT"OF";WE;"POINTS YOU HAVE";WM;"POINTS."
    1565 GOTO 1080
```

The player scores the points when he picks up the gold and
silver coins.   Therefore let us supplement the lines
concerned in our action part:

```
6014 IF N=12 THEN PRINT"O.K.":OB[12]=-1
     :WE=WE+10:GOTO 1080
6017 IF N=17 AND FL[3] THEN PRINT  "O.K.":OB[17]=-
     1:WE=WE+10:GOTO 1080
```

Unfortunately a player who is only trying to score points can achieve sums as high as he likes with the present execution of the program.

Let us remember that on arranging the "Take" action we had agreed that "Take" actually meant to "Take in the hand". In addition to picking up objects for keeping in the inventory, this made it possible in practice to take from the inventory in order to carry out an action, for instance the opening of a door by means of a key.

This interpretation proves to be obstructive, since there is nothing to stop the player from inputting "Take silver coins" several times and adding ten points to his score with this input.

As a way out, either the general preliminary condition (line 6000) can be altered or additional conditions can be introduced into action itself.

We already know this principle from the execution of the "Examine" action. Here a similar arrangement had to be made to prevent an object from repeatedly becoming visible at its place of origin.

```
6014  IF N=12 AND OB[N]=4 THEN PRINT"O.K.":OB[12]=-
      1:WE=WE+10:GOTO 1080
6017  IF  N=17  AND  OB[N]=5  AND  FL[3]  THEN
      PRINT"O.K.":OB[17]=-1:WE=WE+10:GOTO 1080
6020  IF N=12 AND OB[N]=-1 THEN PRINT"I ALREADY HAVE
      THE SILVER !":GOTO 1080
6021  IF N=17 AND OB[N]=-1 THEN PRINT"I AM  ALREADY
      IN THE POSESSION OF THE GOLD!":GOTO 1080
```

On the other hand if you decide always to interpret the "Take" action as an action that makes the player rich, you can restrict yourself to tightening the preliminary condition and outputting a corresponding reference:

```
6000 IF N<>PL THEN GOTO 6900
6998 PRINT"I ALREADY HAVE THAT !":GOTO 1080
```

In the case of our own adventures, or at least the adventures in this book we propose merely scoring the treasures that have come into the player's possession. Even so we shall not be able to do without assessing the player's individual moves.

On the contrary we shall even go a step further and assess each individual player, informing him of the average score obtained.

As a basis for this evaluation the number of moves is available. An experienced adventurer will not linger examining every small thing, just as he knows how to take advantage of typical references.

We work out an average value from this sum and the score achieved and assess the player on the basis of this quotient.

```
180 MOVE=0
1080 PRINT CHR$[154] : MOVE=MOVE+1
1561 PRINT"OF";WM;"POINTS YOU HAVE IN";MOVE;"MOVES"
1562 PRINT SCORE;"POINTS !  THIS EQUALS AN"
1563 PRINT"AVERAGE OF";VALUE/MOVE;"POINTS."
1564 GOTO 1080
```

We also redefine the criterion for a successful end to the game. Instead of a precisely defined condition dependent on the game we now compare the score reached with the maximum value possible. If the difference is nil, the player has solved the problem.

It is expedient to carry out this test right at the start of each move, before any data is passed to the player.

```
1085 IF WM=WE THEN GOTO 4800
```

Should you use the score as a criterion, please do not forget to remove from the program all other lines dealing with the same task [line numbers within the range 1331 to 1389].

With the logical introduction of a points system we are now finally faced with the job of adapting the victory message to this structure.

For that purpose it will of course not be possible to avoid playing through a complete run when the adventure has been completed and contains no more errors. In this game you dispense with all inputs that are not absolutely essential and establish the minimum number of moves required for victory. Calculate the ratio between points and necessary inputs and take this value or a somewhat lower figure as a basis and a characteristic of a very good game.

Choose correspondingly graded remarks for worse assessments.

Thus a game based on the miniversion of Gold Fever can be marked more or less as follows:

```
4800 PRINT CHR$[147]
4805 EW=WE/ZU
4810 PRINT"CONGRATULATIONS"
4810 PRINT"YOU HAVE REACHED THE END OF THE GAME"
4820 PRINT
4825 PRINT"IN";ZUG;"MOVES YOU HAVE SCORED"
4830 PRINT EW;"POINTS"
4835 PRINT"WHICH IS A"
4840 IF EW<0.5 THEN MS$="POOR"
4845 IF EW>0.5 THEN MS$="FAIR"
4850 IF EW>1.0 THEN MS$="GOOD"
4855 IF EW>1.5 THEN MS$="VERY GOOD"
4860 PRINT MS$;"RESULT"
4899 END
```

A title arranged in such a way, suitably made up by the use of control, color, and graphic characters, will induce many adventurers who have finally mastered the adventure to play it again.

These remarks should actually conclude the subject of
"Score". We have to make a technical addition without which
all that lovely planning would be wrecked and whose absence
would definitely disappoint the players of our programs.

Perhaps you have already thought of our Save game routine,
which naturally must be able to store and load the score and
movements introduced above if the player is not repeatedly
to start with zero points.

```
1727 PRINT#2, WE
1728 PRINT#2, MOVE
1827 INPUT#2, WE
1828 INPUT#2, MOVE
```

All suggestions made in this chapter had the sole purpose of
increasing the comfort of the programs.

I think you will agree with me if I say that adventures
developed in accordance with the concept of this book and
contain all the necessary extras may by all means be counted
as belonging to the top class of text adventures. Therefore
let us conclude the technical development with these lines
and turn to the question of how we can make the games
themselves more attractive and even more difficult.

Here we shall do as usual, following dry theory with program
lines intended for our first work, Gold Fever.

The following pages will show you in particular how you can
place further obstacles in the player's way, so that he does
in fact have to make use of the commands Save and Load in
order to get to his goal.

In order to have enough room for monsters, trap doors, and what have you, we shall now deal with the geography again and develop our miniworld so that it provided a basis for a complete adventure.

Should you however intend to enjoy an adventure game yourself, you should, before dealing with the next sections, input all program lines still missing or, better still, have them input by someone else.

A listing with all suggestions made will be found in the last chapter.

4.6 FINDING ONE'S BEARINGS OR LOSING ONE'S BEARINGS

As already mentioned at the beginning of the book, most adventure games are played within a world of about forty spaces. Nevertheless one gets the impression of a much larger world, with the vast woods, a swamp, an underground cave, a maze, and so on.

In actual fact however the extensive-looking areas are small groups of spaces so skillfully interconnected that the player usually does not even notice on what journey he has been sent.

The range of possibilities extends from the plain space that repeatedly leads into itself to a chain of spaces at the end of which the player is returned to start.

Let us at this point make use of the similar spaces 1 and 2 in Gold Fever to have a wide area at our disposal right at the beginning of the game.

Let space 1 lead back into itself again in a northerly and westerly direction, do likewise with space 2, and then try to imagine the player who starts in space 1 and wanders westwards. How is he supposed to know that after each input he is still in the space 1 part of the woods?

Unless he is lucky enough to start the game with the input "E", he will need a series of inputs to find his way out of the woods, which will spoil his chances of a good average on points.

```
501 ... 1,1,1,2,0,0
502 ... 2,2,3,1,0,0
```

The search or the right way will be even more difficult if
the southern exit from space 2 does not cause the player to
go into space 2 again, but causes him to enter space 1.

```
501 ... 1,1,1,2,0,0
502 ... 2,1,1,3,0,0
```

Start the program and see the effect of this small change.

With three spaces it is possible in this way to produce
small mazes if the connections are made at random, without
reference to a compass, and there is only one entrance and
one exit.

The usual connecting technique used by us also keeps to the
real paths predetermined by cardinal points. This creates a
world that permits problem-free identification of the spaces
and enable the player to find his bearings, especially if he
makes a map.

Small jumps over one or two spaces however quickly render
this concept unusable.

Let us imagine three spaces lying one behind the other and
all giving the description "I am in a big cave."

A player who gets into cave 1 from the west will, as he sees
nothing in particular, first want to get to know the
immediate surroundings quickly and presumably will not
change the direction he has taken, since he needs to find
his way back in the easiest possible manner.

After crossing through spaces 2 and 3, he again moves into the first space, but he cannot possibly know this without appropriate action.

By using a jump technique it is possible, without a great deal of work, to produce what appears to be vast mazes. Six spaces are all that is needed to make it almost impossible for the player to find the right way.

Even the programmer will encounter enough difficulties during the test phase!

For even making a map becomes a problem with this method. This is not so with the alternative method briefly described below.

In this case a maze drawn to scale, preferably on squared paper, such as you often find in the puzzle corners of magazines. In the subsequent programming each small box corresponds to a space, so it is possible to see the considerable amount of work involved.

It is likewise easy to see that during his excursion the player takes a new box with each new space, marks the walls, and leaves the passages blank.

Instead take six spaces, in each case using one as an exit space, one as a collecting space, and one as an entry space. In the case of the entry space it is important that it alone leads back to the place last visited and then only in one direction. The same applies to the last space, only one passage allows new territory to be entered, all the other paths lead into the maze.

The collecting space performs a central function. From each
space in the maze two or more paths lead into the collecting
space, but all exits bring the player back into the first or
even the second space in the maze.

To complicate matters further, the exit from the space lying
in front of and connected to the last space is arranged in
such a way that only one path leads into the last space,
while all others lead into the collecting space or the
first space.

Needless to say, an identical description is provided for
all spaces and as far as possible all six directions are
used.   The player will now have to be almost as lucky as a
lottery winner to leave the maze before finding the only
correct path of six in the last space.   Here any mistake
will throw the player back into another space, this in turn
offering six possibilities.

Try to find your way in the following maze.

        The Gold Fever maze:

        110 AR=14
        507 DATA "I AM AT THE ENTRANCE TO A MINE",
        8,0,1,5,0,0
        519 DATA A WINDING TUNNEL,8,0,0,5,0,0
        524 DATA A WINDING TUNNEL,1,0,7,8,8,8,8
        525 DATA A WINDING TUNNEL,11,8,8,13,11,8
        526 DATA A WINDING TUNNEL,11,8,10,11,11,8
        527 DATA A WINDING TUNNEL,9,8,10,11,10,8
        528 DATA A WINDING TUNNEL,8,10,10,11,0,0
        529 DATA A WINDING TUNNEL,0,11,12,11,0,0

4.6.1 CHANGES OF PLACE

Apart from mazes, whatever their size, other means are available to us for making it more difficult for the player to find his bearings.

Sudden transfers of the central figure to another space are very popular. This is made clear to the adventurer by messages such as "Everything around me is turning."

But even this message must be taken at best as a friendly gesture on the part of the programmer and not understood as a duty.

Such actions are usually triggered off by magic objects requiring hard rubbing like Aladdin's magic lamp.

Magic spells and potions prove to be useful, so the player of an adventure program can only be advised to exercise the greatest possible care should the word "magic" be uttered in any connection.

From the programming aspect these changes of place do not cause any kind of difficulty when our adventure system is being used, as all that is necessary is to allocate the number of the space to the variable PL

"Rub lamp" could therefore be implemented as follows [lamp - object 3]:

```
IF N=3 AND OB[3]=1 THEN PRINT
"THE WORLD IS TURNING...":PL=9:GOTO 1080
```

If in addition the description of space 9 is the same as that of the old space, the player probably would inevitably be confused after the next move. This applies particularly to cases in which the messages is omitted or a different text is chosen:

```
IF N=3 AND OB[3]=-1 THEN PRINT
"O.K. - NOTHING HAS HAPPENED.":PL=9:GOTO 1080
```

When the player's change of location is not even dependent on the manipulations of any particular objects, but is governed purely and simply by chance, this means a further increase in the degree of difficulty.

With the construction of our adventure program we can stipulate that a certain space must be crossed. If the contents of PL correspond to the number of this space, a chance decision is made as to whether the player is to be transferred or whether for the purpose of execution of other actions he is to be allowed to stay.

What player who after sucessfully crossing a maze and then entering an apparently harmless space is more than once thrown back into the maze will take the risk of a repetition of this?

Another extract from the Gold Fever adventure shows how this handicap can be built in:

```
110 NS=16
519 DATA IN A WINDING PASSAGE. ,8,0,15,5,0,0
521 DATA IN A TUNNEL. ,0,15,0,0,0,0
1340 IF PL=15 THEN IF RND[1]> .7 THEN SP=16
```

The player is transferred to the critical space by leaving the entrance to the maze, at present space eight, a winding passage, in a westerly direction.

He can withdraw from this space immediately or try to find out what the wider surroundings hold in store for him.

If chance will have it (and whether he wants to we establish with the comparative value in the RND function), he gets into the next space [16]. If not, he finds himself again in a space in the maze (collecting space 11), but this space offers no clues that will help him to find his bearings.

Unless fortune smiles on him, he will decide after a few attempts that it is another entrance to the maze. He will then avoid this space and so never find some of the treasure.

4.6.2 HIDDEN ENTRANCES

These can cause the player at least as much difficulty. Even if in the line "I can go ..." only the directions east and west are mentioned, the world does not have to end in the north:

```
    I SEE A DARK ROCK CAVE,
    A FEROCIOUS-LOOKING BEAR,
    **NUGGETS**.
    I CAN GO WEST, EAST.
    ----------------------------------
```

```
    O.K.
    WHAT AM I TO DO?  E
    O.K.
    WHAT AM I TO DO?  S
    O.K.
    WHAT AM I TO DO?  W
    O.K.
    WHAT AM I TO DO?  EXAMINE CAVE
    I HAVE STARTLED A BEAR.
    WHAT AM I TO DO?  N
```

Many players, if they are beginners, or indeed most will rely on the details given and never enter the cave, since any suspicion of a large-scale cave world is immediately dispelled by the fact that it is possible to explore the cave and carry out other actions.

Only an input such as "Enter cave" will lead to fresh discoveries:

```
130 AV=7
209 DATA ENTER
2200 ON VN GOTO 5000,6000,7000,8000,9000,10000,13000
13010 IF N=13 AND PL=5 THEN PL=12:
      PRINT "O.K.": GOTO 1080
```

NOTE: Before you satisfy yourself as to the function of those lines, it is essential to input all further spaces and also to alter the connections of those already existing [lines 500 -700].

Line 110 must be adapted to the new situation.

The nice thing about this is that the entrance is not even camouflaged.

It is now no longer the player's task merely to track down a hidden space and enter this by means of correctly chosen words, but he must be able to develop a plan of how a usable path leading to the space can be constructed.

Taking the simplest case, a door will be involved, a door that is initially locked. An indication by the driver is ensured by the descriptions of the objects and by the data in the line of the direction table applicable to this space:

```
xxxx DATA A DOOR, DOOR, 1

xxxx REM SPACE 1
xxxx DATA IN A CELL.,0,0,0,0,0,0
```

With this the usual procedure is that the player on examining the cell discovers the door, which carries a massive lock. "Open door" and "Open lock" point to the missing key, so the player feels compelled to check all other objects in the space to see whether they can be used for opening the lock.

In most adventures the mere presence of the key in the inventory is enough, while others demand some appropriate use of the key, a feature that we can now explain in light of our practical experience.

While some are content with a simple text, the other, more elaborate programs use flags as well [OB][N]=-1.

However, once the door is open, an appropriate indication of direction appears within the heading line and from this we manipulate the array item PASSAGE [r,ri] relevant to this space.

```
xxxx IF N=y AND OB[z]=-1 AND PL=x
     THEN PRINT O.K.":PA[r,ri]=nr : GOTO 1080
```

    y = object number door
    z = object number key
    r = present space
    ri= cardinal point concerned
    nr= new space to be reached

The above line, inserted into the program deals with the verb "OPEN", this makes sure that the player is in possession of the right key [z] and is standing in front of the right door [r]. Then the details in the direction table are altered accordingly.

4.7 LIMITATIONS AND COUNTERS

I regard these as especially suitable for giving prominence to a particular adventure in relation to all the rest, since after all they give every adventure problem the fascination of reality and make some selections of the adventure real brain teasers.

Their function is seen not so much in the active participation of the game but as a background check for the general conditions on which the game is based.

At this point it is probably necessary to mention the restriction imposed on the inventory, since a weight limit is now one of the things that create reality in adventure games.

Assuming that we are not dealing with a superhuman adventure, it would in the first place be unbelievable that one person could drag about an unlimited number of objects. In the second place the game can become too easy if all the objects used in the action are available immediately.

Technically, a counter monitors the number of pieces that the player is carrying with him and if he is already carrying the maximum load provided for by the programmer, he will refuse to pick up any more objects.

Therefore, before any action is begun, the maximum number of pieces allowed must be established:

    185 IMAX=5

Otherwise we leave the inventory routine as it is, since it is the action of TAKEing which we must pay closer attention. All actions involving the verb "Take" will now be based on a further common condition, so for the second time an alteration to line 6000 is called for.

Regrettably this planning not only provides for a restructuring of the block concerned, but also destroys our dream of a universally usable driver with all functions and restrictions.

For this reason we alter the jump table in line 2200 and implement the necessary text before starting the actual execution of the commands:

```
2200 ON VN GOTO 5000,2210,7000,8000,9000,10000
2201 REM TEST FOR ROOM IN THE INV
2210 NUMBER=0
2220 FOR I=1 TO AO
2230 IF OB[I]=-1 THEN NUMBER=NUMBER+1
2240 IF NUMBER=IMAX THEN PRINT "NO, THANKS. -
     I AM ALREADY CARRYING ENOUGH !":GOTO 1080
2250 NEXT I
2260 GOTO 6000 : REM EXECUTION TAKE --
2270 REM ----------- END OF INV TEST
```

While this counter plays a passive role and the routine is called up only within the limits of a precisely defined action, other background checks not only restrict the player's freedom of action, but may even lead to the end of the game.

4.8 AVAILABLE LIGHT

This is an expression commonly used in some adventure programs to describe a feature that causes additional difficulties that can drive the players to despair.

For players who have a passion for adventure games the usual obstacles do not seem to be enough, and since it is a well known fact that there is nothing more difficult than life in the everyday world, the only thing that can be done to overcome this unbearable condition is to imitate this world more perfectly.

Without light we are in the dark and shall hardly be able to see anything, yet act properly. If we add to this the fact that we are not in our bedroom, where this condition would be far less of an obstacle, but in a wild and fissured rocky landscape, any further step becomes a deadly risk.

Naturally this is just what we adventure producers want, and when we build the next lines into our adventures, we shall get additional pleasure from imagining the reactions of our friends, to whom of course we want to present our work.

Fortunately every adventure program can have this obstacle built in. Often big caves or underground systems of passageways are available, while other programs take place in a house; these are all places that need artificial lighting. Should it in fact ever happen that the entire action takes place in the open air, the movement of the earth in relation to the sun must be followed.

In order to be able to realize a sunrise and sunset, all
that it is necessary to do is to use another counter.

First we determine how long the day or night is to last,
using the player's inputs as a unit of time.

Let us assume that the night begins 50 moves after sunrise.
This value will be just as typical of any adventure as the
number of attainable points, so the corresponding variable
LM [amount of light] is initialized at the start of the
program:

        186 LM=50 : LIGHT=-1

Your extensive knowledge of the subject of adventure will
allow you to interpret the variable LIGHT as a signal
switch, in the sense that a -1 means as adequate amount of
light for all actions, but 0 absolute darkness.

The two possible positions of this switch show the output
routine of our driver whether the player can see anything or
whether he has to tap his way forward in the dark:

        1131 REM ------------------------------ NO LIGHT
        1132 IF LIGHT THEN 1140
        1133 PRINT"I DO NOT KNOW EXACTLY WHERE I AM."
        1134 PRINT"IT IS TOO DARK TO SEE ANYTHING."
        1135 PRINT: PRINT:"I CAN NO LONGER SEE THE EXITS
             EITHER.":GOTO 1330

After line 1132 the output routines used so far will be used
if there is any light.

If there is no light, lines 1133 to 1135 state in the usual
way that there is nothing to be seen.

We have only to see that the LIGHT switch is in its correct
position; this has to be done after completion of the number
of moves fixed with LM.

The move counter cannot be used for this comparison
operation,   because   a day-to-night change necessitates
resetting the counter to zero; let us therefore introduce
the variable LIGHT CHANGE [LW]:

```
186 LM=50 : LIGHT=-1 : LW=0
1080 MOVE=MOVE+1 : LW=LW+1
1084 IF LW=LM THEN GOSUB 3000
2999 REM SUBROUTINE LIGHT SWITCH
3000 IF LIGHT=-1 THEN LIGHT=0
3010 IF LIGHT=0 THEN LIGHT=-1
3020 LW=0
3030 RETURN
```

At the beginning of any new round of inputs a check is made
to   see   whether   the   duration [LM] specified for   any
particular period has been reached.   If so, the SWITCH
subroutine is called up and the condition of LIGHT changed.
No more than that is required to expose the adventurer to a
day-and-night change, which may necessitate searching for a
lamp.

In the case of Gold Fever however let us not be content with
simulating the movement of the earth in relation to the sun,
but make the event dependent on the possession of a lamp.

Because of this we set the player the additional task of always keeping enough fuel available for the source of light. In our case the fuel will be oil, which the player can find in the bear's cave. In the cave he pours the oil into the bottle, which he must already have taken, and then into the lamp.

Each filling operation resets the LIGHT CHANGE counter to to maximum value.

To make the matter more complicated, the lamp will still contain some oil when the player finds it. If then he goes into the depths of the mine without topping up the lamp, he will be lost without any chance of rescue. One more step, and the adventurer stumbles and breaks his neck.

Since we have not allowed for any darkness in the rest of the territory, the first step needed to realize this version is to alter the starting values.

A switch is made only when the LIGHT CHANGE counter equals the contents of the amount of light.

However, in order to allow the player an almost unlimited number of moves, we fix LM at zero and LW at one, thus making certain that LW can never equal LM:

    186 LM=0 : LIGHT=-1 : LW=1 : L1=20

L1 is added because the existing filling is supposed to be less than the subsequent toppings up. The remaining lines can be taken from the previous example.

This routine is activated only when the lamp is first lit. In addition to the output of "O.K." the execution of this command will correctly initialize the counters as well

```
11030 IF N-23 AND OB[23]=-1 THEN PRINT
      "O.K. - THE LAMP IS ALIGHT."
      :LM=L1:LW=1:GOTO 1080
```

The player now has enough light available for the next twenty actions. By topping up the lamp, he can increase this figure to fifty:

```
12010 IF N=23 AND OB[23]=-1 AND PL[6]
      THEN L1=50:LM=50:LW=1:PRINT
      "O.K.":GOTO 1080
```

To make it possible to top up the supply of fuel with the lamp both on and off, we allocate the number of moves that can now be made to the variables L1 and LM.

In case the player comes to the surface or puts out the lamp for other reasons we must save the present "tank contents":

```
210   DATA EXTINGUISH
14000 IF N-23 AND OB[23]=-1 THEN L1=LM-LW
      :PRINT "O.K.": GOTO 1080
```

Likewise these values must be saved when a game is stored:

```
1625 PRINT #2,PL:PRINT #2,L1:PRINT #2,LM:
     PRINT #2,LW
1725 INPUT #2,PL:INPUT #2,L1:INPUT #2, LM:
     INPUT #2,LW
```

In this way we have made sure that the matter of the light
really has to follow the course set out for it.

However, in order to save the player the sudden, unpleasant
surprise of an inevitable end, it is only fair to give him a
warning, since if he should find himself in the depths of
the earth while the oil is running out, he will no longer be
able to save his skin.

The following line will inform him of the impending danger
shortly before the fuel in the lamp runs out:

```
1350 IF LM-LW>=15 THEN PRINT "THE LIGHT FROM THE
"LAMP IS GETTING WEAKER."
```

By using another counter, you can make reactions dependent
on the time elapsed.

4.9 INCIDENTS

Earthquakes causing an avalanche of rocks, monsters that suddenly appear, the natural enemies of the central figure in the adventure, or even trap doors that open at the wrong moment are other, universally popular things calculated to get the player off the right track.

Nearly always such events are governed by chance and in two respects.

A monster can liven up a certain space and tear off the player's head:

```
1360   IF  PL=10 THEN NS$(0)="THIS TIME  I  HAD  NO
HONEY FOR THE BEAR." :GOTO 4500
```

In just the same way the trap door may only sometimes open and at other times not harm a hair of the player's head:

```
1370 IF PL=20 AND RND(1)>.8 THEN MS$(0)=
        "THE GROUND CAVED IN UNDER ME.":GOTO 4500
```

The third version is a combination of the elements already presented. It may also be assumed that the adventurer's enemies move around, so a certain section of the adventure world should be placed at the monster's disposal as a playground:

```
1380 IF (PL=13 OR PL=14 OR PL=16) AND RND(1)>.8
        THEN MS$(0)="THE BEAR AGAIN.":GOTO 4500
```

4.10 FROM TEXT TO GRAPHICS ADVENTURE

In addition to the features discussed, adventure programs
recently introduced usually have an outstanding graphic
presentation. For each space in the adventure there is a
picture on the disk that when required is loaded into the
computer screen memory.

To produces such elaborate graphics and integrate them into
our adventure system will not be possible for us without
some aids. Even so at this point we are going to suggest a
way of making your programs more attractive.

Presumably you too have often regretted the fact that the
Commodore 64 - Basic contains no commands for making Hires
pictures. Therefore you have the choice of using a BASIC
extension such as VIDEO BASIC from ABACUS SOFTWARE or the
graphics characters that can be input via the keyboard.

Both solutions necessitate a few small alterations to our
driver program, since the outputs now have to be made at
other points of the screen.

Presumably you too will prefer to restrict the text output
to the lower part of the monitor picture. For this purpose
you must alter all lines of the driver that position the
cursor [1070,1080,1090,1130,1390] and you must do that by
poking the new line number into storage position 214. When
using VIDEO BASIC, select suitable co-ordinates for the TEXT
command.

You leave the structure of the particular graphics concerned
to a number of subroutines called up from the driver. It

should however be noted that this printing routine does not
have to be called up after every input made by the   player,
so we introduce a further check variable:

```
     1143 IF ALT<>PL THEN PRINT CHR$[147]:GOSUB 30000
     1145 ALT=PL
```

After a space has been drawn its number is passed on to the
variable ALT.   If the player moves into another space, the
condition in the line 1143 is fulfilled, the screen is
cleared, and line 30000 is called up. This line selects the
correct character routine on the basis of the space number:

```
     30000 ON PL GOSUB 31000,32000,33000
     30010 RETURN
     31000 REM SPACE 1
     31999 RETURN
     32000 REM SPACE 2
     31999 RETURN
```

After this the program is continued with the rest of the
command.

5. THE ADVENTURE EDITOR

The preceding chapters have provided you with the necessary tools for writing good adventures. Even so, although with our system we have developed a concept that for the development of different kinds of adventures necessitates only the programming of the data, conditions, and actions involved in the game concerned, a considerable amount of work is necessary before an attempt at a game can begin.

The job would be simplified by using what is called an adventure generator, which, when all the necessary data have been input, leaves behind on the disk a finished, ready-to-play program.

This solution still requires that the planning of the game has been completed, since before the generator can start the adventure producer has to prepare a list of all ROOMS, objects, verbs, etc and then input this data in a mammoth session.

If any errors come to light while the program thus produced is being tested, they must be rectified in the usual way.

Therefore a far more desirable solution would be one that immediately records every individual thought of the author and moreover immediately checks it and improves it.

This however can happen only if instead of producing a finished program a file is developed containing all the necessary data for a game to be played. The evaluation of this data then becomes the job of an interpreter containing the routines required for execution of all kinds of actions.

5.1 THE FILE

It has already been made clear that the actual adventure is now represented only by a file. This must contain all details necessary to a given game in a precisely defined order, so that the interpreter is able to read various adventures of different length.

If we make a close examination of one of the adventures we have programmed, it is seen that many of the adventures already work interpretively.

The verbs, like the objects, are not called on directly to execute an action, but first two numbers are ascertained whose combination establishes exactly what input the player has made.

As a prerequisite to this method of working, it was essential to read the words into variables, a process that instead of using the data lines can make direct use of the file on a disk [cassette].

We have already also ascertained the data typical of games and entered them into the program in lines 100 to 200 as characteristics of the adventure.

Let us now consider what values from this block are necessary for an interpreter that, while not containing all the extras offered by one system, does offer a sufficient number of functions to make a game possible.

First we find some information on the number of existing rooms, objects, and verbs. These limiting values prove necessary for correct control of the reading-in loops and for the same reason will be necessary for the interpreter. We shall also have to fix the exact number of all messages, since they will be kept in variables.

The same applies to the conditions and actions. In a field similar to the direction table PA[,] we shall keep the playing data ready for reading so we add the variables AC and BC [action codes and condition codes] to the list of characteristics.

Now we must include the number of flags, since our interpreter must be able to store the score.

As another value important to the game, we must include the player's starting position in the file. It is true, the functioning of the system would still be ensured even if PL were not initialized at the start of the game, but then every adventure would always have to begin in space 1. At first sight there is no disadvantage to this, but just imagine if after some slight change in the action the adventurer is to start the game at some completely different place. If then there is no PL variable that can be reinitialized accordingly, you must rewrite all space descriptions in accordance with the new planning.

We cannot dispense with a score by points. However, in order that the end of the game may be defined, we shall provide for an action that can evaluate the flags or the objects in the inventory.

It is recommended that name of the author, the name of the adventure, and version number be kept in the file.

5.2 THE STRUCTURE OF THE EDITOR

The task of the editor is to make it possible for the user
to input this data and, if necessary, alter it in a
convenient and clear way. For this purpose a number of
program lines will be called up through a menu.

Here the sequence will to a certain extent be predetermined,
for so long as the spaces do not yet exist, the objects
cannot be placed. The menu screen for the construction of an
adventure with the editor could look like this:

```
ADVENTURE EDITOR           VER i.O
------------------------------------------------------------
      0 - DATA
      1 - INPUT SPACES
      2 - INPUT OBJECTS
      3 - INPUT VERBS
      4 - OBJECT POSITIONS
      5 - CONNECT SPACES
      6 - CONDITIONS & ACTIONS
      7 - INPUT MESSAGES
      8 - DISK ACCESS
      9 - PROGRAM END
------------------------------------------------------------
         PLEASE CHOOSE
```

The user chooses the function required by inputting the
appropriate number, so, following the commands needed for
the above picture, we provide the jump line:

```
    240 ON A GOTO 1100,1200,1300,1400,1500,
          1600,4000,5000
```

5.2.1 THE INPUTS

Before we start structuring the individual subroutines, the
following will help us to keep the amount of work involved
as small as possible and the editor short.

The user must always be informed of the data expected, so
that he may make correct inputs. To help you we construct
some simple input masks containing appropriate references.
These masks will be largely identical, at least when the
ROOMS, objects, and verbs are input, so a common program
section is indicated for these jobs.

In order that this subroutine may give the correct
instructions, the following titles must be made available
before calling the subroutine:

```
1100 PRINT CHR$[147]:T1$-"INPUT PLACES"
:T2$-"ROOM NO.":T3$-"I AM"
1105 Z=NS
1110 GOSUB 510
```

Following this the number of existing ROOMs is communicated
to the variable Z and the input/output mask is called
[LINE 1110].

To structure the mask, the cursor must repeatedly be
positioned at other points in the manner already explained.

However, in order not to make the program difficult to read
with a lot of POKE instructions, we provide for a further
subroutine that sets the cursor to the requires line and
column:

```
11000 POKE 211,ZE:POKE 214,SP:SYS 58732:RETURN
499   REM ------ I/O ROUTINE
500   PRINT "*";
510   ZE=0SP=0:GOSUB 11000: PRINT T1$
520   Z=Z+1
555   ZE=0:SP=25:GOSUB 11000:PRINT T2$;Z
556   PRINT M3$
557   ZE=16:SP=0:GOSUB 11000:PRINT M4$
558   ZE=16:SP=0:GOSUB 11000:PRINTZ-1;:  IF A=1 THEN
PRINT RE$[Z-1]
559   IF A=2 THEN PRINT OB$[Z-1]
560   IF A=3 THEN PRINT VERB$[Z-1]
563   ZE=20:SP=0:GOSUB 11000:PRINT3$;:EI$="":INPUTEI$
564   IF LEFT$[EI$,1]="*"THEN GOTO 200
565   IF  A=2  THEN  ZE+22:SP=0:GOSUB   11000:INPUT
"OBJECT NAME ";RN$[Z]
570   ZE=20:SP=0:GOSUB 11000:PRINT M4$
571   ZE=22:SP=0:GOSUB 11000:PRINT M4$
590   RETURN
```

First the appropriate references are printed out. In lines
558 to 560 a check made on the value in A that establishes
what data to be input is involved. Then, as a reminder, the
last previously input word is printed.

Line 568 accepts the input, and the allocation to the
correct variable is made within the calling subroutines
(with the exception of the second object name, which is
input in line 565). Lines 570 to 571 delete the input lines
and so prevent values previously input from being taken at
the next input. The function called up is ended by line 564
after an asterisk has been input. The object and verbs are
input as in this example.

5.2.2 SPACE CONNECTIONS

First it is necessary to indicate all possible spaces, so that the user may input the correct space numbers. Since this function is necessary for placing the objects, we construct a further subroutine [12000 -12070].

Then for all spaces the six directions are interrogated in turn and the inputs written directly into the corresponding position of the direction table:

```
1499 REM ---------------------- CONNECT SPACES
1500 FOR R1-12 TO AR
1520 GOSUB 12000
1530 PRINT "SPACE";R1;"LEADS NORTH INTO SPACE";
        :INPUT DU[R1,1]
1540 PRINT "SPACE";R1;"LEADS SOUTH INTO SPACE";
        :INPUT DU[R1,2]
1585 NEXT R1
1590 GOTO 200
1591 REM ---------------------- END OF CONNECTIONS
```

5.2.3 ACTIONS & CONDITIONS

Before we proceed to input the more important data, the
conditions and actions, we must develop a coding system.

For keeping the data we use a two-dimensional array. This
time the rows are predetermined by the verbs and the columns
by the objects.

To make it easy to interpret the conditions, we decide on
coding by letters. It is true numbers would have the
advantage of speed in processing, but it is certainly more
difficult to recognize the significance of a twelve digit
figure than to interpret a string such as RF3S22 if
conventions have been observed as seen in the following
illustrations.

```
PLEASE INPUT ALL CONDITIONS FOR THE ACTION
"EXAMINE DOOR"
-------------------------------------------


     R     - OBJECT IS IN THE SPACE
     I     - OBJECT IS IN THE INVENTORY
     N     - OBJECT IS NOT AVAILABLE
     FX    - FLAG X IS SET
     GX    - FLAG X IS DELETED
     SXX   - PLAYER IS IN SPACE XX


-------------------------------------------
OLD CODE ===>
CONDITIONS?  RSO2
```

These conditions are perfectly adequate when is comes to ensuring that the player's actions cannot be carried out except at the times prescribed by the plot.

The actions provided for are also essentially in accordance with the ides from the previous chapters. The only new thing added is the commands Dxxy and E.

The command D is intended to cause the interpreter to make visible an exit from the present space to space xx in the direction y.   E ends the game and informs the player of his victory.

```
     RS02 FULFILLED, THE FOLLOWING ACTION:
--------------------------------------------------------
     V    - DOOR DISAPPEARS
     I    - DOOR COMES INTO THE INVENTORY
     NXX  - OBJECT XX REAPPEARS
     DXXY - PASSAGE TO ROOM XX DIR. Y
     SXX  - PLAYER TO SPACE XX
     FX   - SET FLAG X
     LX   - DELETE FLAG X
     MXX  - OUTPUT MESSAGE XX
     T    - PLAYER DIES
     E    - END, PLAYER HAVING WON
--------------------------------------------------------
     OLD CODE --->
     ACTION?    M09
```

5.2.4 THE MESSAGES

These can be written into the correct variables without
further ado immediately on inputting. The program part
provided turns out to be correspondingly short:

```
3999 REM --------------------------- COMMUNICATIONS
4000 PRINT "INPUT COMMUNICATIONS"
4010 PRINT M3$
4020 AM-AM+1
4030 PRINT AM: INPUT MS$[AM]
4040 IF LEFT$[MS$[AM]="*" THEN AM=AM-1: GOTO 200
4050 GOTO 4020
4060 REM ------------------- END OF COMMUNICATIONS
```

AM keeps a check on the number of messages input and, on
completion of the function, must be reduced by one when
inputting as asterisk.

5.2.5 DISK ACCESSES

This is necessary for storing the file or for reloading it into the computer for reprocessing. In order that the file be available for rebuilding by the interpreter, even if a game has not yet been fully completed, additional data must be input before any storage operation.

What is above all important to the interpreter is the word length, since the interpreter is not supposed to occupy any more memory than is necessary.

As already mentioned, the player's starting space must be contained in the file, just as the number of flags used becomes important to the interpreter as soon as the SAVE GAME function is called up.

After these values have been input, all the data is placed on the disk as a sequential file. Cassette users are asked to note the changes given in the previous chapter.

Otherwise the listing of the adventure editor has no peculiarities, so you should understand the method of operation, due to to the individual blocks, and be able to expand the program as you wish.

5.3 THE ADVENTURE INTERPRETER

Understanding the interpreter itself will not cause you any difficulty, since, like our adventure programs, it is built up from three blocks.

In the first part of the program the variables are again initialized with the data necessary for the game. Instead of the DATA lines with the relevant READ instructions we now use a data file produced with the editor.

After you have selected the file required, it is evaluated and entered from line 50 to line 200.

The program block from line 1000 up to and including line 2160 corresponds to the driver developed by us. No alterations are necessary.

Entirely new however is the method of carrying out the actions.

A single program, the interpreter, is supposed to enable different games to be played. Therefore it is not possible to use rigid structures always tailored to only one given situation. From a series of individual actions, those necessary to the particular case concerned are picked out and carried out until the sum of their effects has achieved the same result.

We pursue this strategy both when checking the conditions and when carrying out the actions.

```
2200 FOR AB=1 TO LEN[BC$[VN,N]]
2210 RD$[AB]=MID$[BC$[VN,N],AB,1]
2220 NEXT AB
```

First the final value of the loop is ascertained, this being dependent on the number of letters used for coding a particular action.   Then the entire string is split up into the individual conditions, each of these being allocated to one element of the list BD$[].

A further loop now checks the fulfillment of each individual condition within a further loop.

On coding, however, it was necessary to fix two or more parameters for some of the conditions.   Thus code S [presence of the player in a specific space] requires an indication of the space number, just as in the case of F and G the flag concerned has to be named.

For these reasons we dispense with a For/Next loop and instead select a structure that allows us to increase the loop counter by differing values of our choice.

In addition to this variable [K] we use a further variable [RESULT] that after each execution of the loop is supposed to be logically true [-1], if the condition has been fulfilled, and then on leaving the loop will be logically no [0] if only one condition is fulfilled.

```
2300 X=0:ER=0
```

Each execution of the loop must begin with raising the counter.   Immediately thereafter a check is made to see

whether the final value, which of course is dependent on the
number of conditions, has or has not been reached.

```
2310 X=X+1
2320 IF X=AB+1 THEN 2500 :REM ALL CONDITIONS CHECKED
```

Depending on ER, it is now decided whether a reaction takes
place or whether the player has to carry out further
preparatory actions.

```
2500  IF NOT ER THEN PRINT"THAT CANNOT BE DONE  AT
PRESENT.":GOTO 1080
3999 REM ----- ALL CONDITIONS FULFILLED
4000 PRINT "O,K."
```

Within the loop body the conditions are checked one after
the other, the program line concerned being ascertained in
the same way as, for example, the routines for handling the
one-word commands within our driver program:

```
2330 IF BD$[X]<>"R"THEN 2350
2340 IF OB[N]<>SP THEN ER=-1 :GOTO 2310
2350 IF BD$[X]<>"I"THEN 2370
2360 IF  OB[N]<>-1 THEN ER=-1 : GOTO 2310
2370 IF BD$[X]<>"N" THEN 2390
2380 IF  [OB[N]<>SP AND OB[N]<>-1] THEN  ER=-1  :
GOTO 2310
2390 IF BD$[X]<>"S" THEN 2410
2400 R1$=BD$[X+1]+BD$[X+2]:X=X+2:  IF SP=VAL[R1$]
THEN ER=-1 : GOTO 2310
2410 IF BD$[X]<>"F" THEN 2450
2420 IF FL[VAL[BD$[X+1]]]=-1THEN 2440
2430 X=X+1:GOTO2450
```

```
2440 ER=-1:X=X+1:GOTO 2310
2450 IF BD$[X]<>"G" THEN 2310
2460 IF NOT FL[VAL[BD$[X+1]]] THEN 2480
2470 X=X+1:GOTO 2310
2480 ER=-1:X=X+1:GOTO 2310
2490 GOTO 2310
```

Apart from lines 2400 to 2470 these lines will not present you with any kind of problem. In line 2400 the next two elements of the condition code BD$ are also called upon in order to ascertain the space number. Then the counter is adjusted and, if necessary, the result variable set to true.

The lines provided for evaluation of the flags work in a similar way. The program lines executing a command work in an identical manner.

Within this block attention need be drawn only to lines 5200 to 5290, which, for example, make it possible to open a door. By manipulating these lines, the correct values are written into the direction table, so that on the one hand the new passage becomes visible [5220], while on the other there is a way back if the player has moved into the new space [5230 to 5290].

Lines 5500 to 5700 each contain a short subroutine that serves to determine a two-digit figure [5500], a single figure [5600], or two figures [5700]. These values are needed for outputting the correct messages and the correct handling of the flags and for opening a passage to a specific flag in one of the six directions.

Please obtain the complete listings from the next chapter.

6. ADVENTURE PRACTICE

This chapter will not show you so much how you do something as what you can do.

You will find the complete listings of two adventures that have been written using the program parts and routines developed in this book and also operating instructions for the software printed below.

One of the adventures, is called Gold Fever, an adventure of which already quite enough has been said. The other is The Enchanted Castle, an adventure program for whose solution we shall not give any information of any kind.

Unfortunately however the position is that when you have worked through this book you will be able to read the programs almost like set of instructions for solving them. Therefore it is recommended that you share the job of typing them in with someone.

This applies in particular to the program lines starting at number 5000, as here the action is programmed.

Then you will find two shorter programs involving an adventure editor and its interpreter.

Both programs together enable you to produce menu-controlled adventures and to play them from the very first step in the development of the story.

6.1 INSTRUCTIONS FOR PLAYING ADVENTURES

After you have started the program with RUN, the first descriptions and communications will appear on the monitor following the header picture and other general notes on playing.

You must distinguish between the upper and lower halves of the screen: In the upper half you will find a description of the place in which you happen to be. Directly below all visible objects are listed, and another line indicates the direction in which you can move. The lower half is used for inputting your commands to the program and for outputting to you the information dependent on the execution of your input.

6.1.1 YOUR INPUTS:

Your usual inputs will consist of two words, a verb and an object. See that you use designations that are the same as output in the upper part of the screen.

This does not however mean that following a communication such as

        I CAN SEE A RED DOOR.
        WHAT AM I TO DO?

You react with OPEN RED DOOR. Usually the input OPEN DOOR will be perfectly adequate.

In addition you will be allowed a few further inputs,
commands known as one-word commands, which permit certain
functions that, while not being absolutely essential to the
game, simplify it.

6.1.2 THREE-DIMENSIONAL PROGRAMS

Generally you can always move in the directions indicated.
For this purpose it is sufficient to input the initial
letter of the direction concerned: north, south, east, west
[N,S,E,W] and up or down [U or D].

These are however exceptions, and sometimes an input such as
ENTER... can be used to good effect.

6.1.3 MANIPULATION OF OBJECTS

Naturally you want to do more in the imaginary world than go
on a sightseeing tour: you want to act and solve a problem.

For this purpose you must first discover the objects in this
picture world. Then you can EXAMINE them, TAKE them, USE
them, etc. [If you are ever stuck, you should remember
these words!].

Let us assume you find a key. You think: "Great, but what
am I to do with it?"

In real life you would look at it, examine it carefully, and
then decide whether you are going to leave it or whether you

consider it to be useful or even valuable and therefore whether you are going to take it with you. You should follow this logical course of events in the adventure.

Input: EXAMINE KEY. In answer you may get: IT IS THE KEY TO MY HOUSE or: IT IS A CAR KEY or: IT IS MADE OF PURE GOLD. Naturally you would not leave any of these keys behind, but would take them all with you, so input: TAKE KEY. The communication then appearing on the screen is an O.K. [You will often see this O.K.; it means that the adventure interpreter has understood and executed your input.]. Furthermore the key will no longer appear in the heading line I SEE, since, as you have taken it, it is now in your coat pocket [or somewhere else on your person], but no longer in the space.

If in the course of the game you have accumulated a lot of objects in your pockets, you will probably lose count, so the interpreter offers you the possibility of making an INVENTORY. Whenever you want to know for example whether you are carrying anything around with you that would help you to solve a particular problem, you simply input INV. the answer that immediately appears is: I AM CARRYING THE FOLLOWING ITEMS. A list of all the objects concerned then follows.

6.1.4 INTERRUPTION OF PLAY:

You will probably not be able to solve an adventure in one day, and naturally you do not want to start all over again the next day. Therefore you will need the possibility of storing your progress so far.

If you want to end a game temporarily, you simply input SAVE. The interpreter then asks you for a name under which it is to store the latest situation.

Storing the current stage of your progress is actually recommended at sometimes. For example it could happen that you want to climb a step rockface, but are wearing the wrong sort of footwear. It is highly probable that you will fall and break your neck. Then you would have to start all over again and repeat all your inputs, a job that timely storage of the game would have saved you.

6.1.5 CONTINUING AN INTERRUPTED GAME:

When you have stored the situation, you simply input LOAD. The interpreter then asks you under what name you stored the game and, following depression of the <RETURN> key, continues the game from the point at which it was interrupted.

6.1.6 OTHER INFORMATION:

When you play an adventure, you must first find out what
sort of adventure it is. You have either to solve a
problem, look for an exit or collect treasures. You should
first EXAMINE everything and act as logically as possible
[thus to OPEN a LOCKED DOOR you first need a KEY, a CROWBAR,
or something similar]. If you are on the right path, the
interpreter will let you know this with a message such as
THAT CANNOT BE DONE AT PRESENT or I DO NOT UNDERSTAND WHAT
YOU MEAN.

These messages signify that the words used in your input
have been understood, but not all the conditions necessary
for execution of the action have yet been fulfilled [for
instance the KEY is missing].

If a verb or the object is not understood, you will be
informed and you should try to reach the same goal with
other words.

O.K. is a signal to you that an input has been understood
and that a reaction has taken place. Mostly the lower
half of the screen will display other messages that describe
the reaction more accurately.

6.2 TIPS ON HOW TO SOLVE AN ADVENTURE

If you are completely stuck in a given situation, you can first try HELP.

If you do not get more information by doing this, recall all the objects so far discovered. Almost certainly each object has a job allotted to it; to use it only to decorate a space would involve too much programming work.

Here, a list of all words understood by the program would be useful; this could possibly be drawn up for you from the adventure itself, following the command VOCabulary.

Equally useful would be a map on which you enter all the spaces with their connections, naturally not forgetting the places where the objects were found.

In the case of a maze, however, making such a map is not quite as easy as you may imagine.

Instead of only spaces that really exist, one has often mapped three times that number. The only trick that can be used to avoid this is to deposit one object from the inventory in each space of the maze, thus making it impossible to get the individual locations mixed up.

And as a final bit of advice:

In between times store your game over and over again!

6.3 PROGRAM LISTINGS

The following pages contain the program listings:

        1.   GOLDER FEVER
        2.   THE ENCHANTED CASTLE
        3.   ADVENTURE EDITOR
        4.   ADVENTURE INTERPRETER

The programs were listed with a TURBOPRINT GT printer interface in the special listing mode. Please see Appendix A for a complete description of the listing codes.

The listings in this book are available on a ready to run 1541 Diskette. By purchasing this diskette, you can eliminate typing thes programs into your Commodore 64.

The programs on the diskette have been fully tested and are available for $14.95 + $2.00 [$5.00 foreign] postage and handling charge.

To order send name, address, and a check, money order or credit card information to:

ABACUS SOFTWARE

P.O. BOX 7211

GRAND RAPIDS, MI 49510

Or call [616]-241-5510 for the name of your nearest dealer.

Be sure to ask for the "Optional Diskette for the Adventure Gamewriter's Handbook".

```
1 REM -- GOLD FEVER, VERSION 1.0 --
2 REM     [C] 1984 BY WALKOWIAK
10 REM ---------------------- TITLE PIC
TURE
11 POKE53281,11:POKE53280,12:PRINTCHR$[1
42]
12 PRINT"{CLR}"
13 PRINT"{CM5}                      {CM+
}{CM+}{CM+}{CM+}{CM+}{CM+}{CM+}{CM+}{CM+
}{CM+}{CM+}{CM+}{CM+}{CM+}{CM+}
14 PRINT"{YEL}    {SHO}{CMY} {SHO}{SHP} {
CMG}  {SHO}{SHM} {BLK}{SHO}{CMY} {SHO}{C
MY} {CMG}{CMM} {SHO}{CMY} {SHO}{SHP}{CM5
}{CM+}{CM+}{CM+}{CM+}{CM+}{CM+}{CM+}{CM+
}
15 PRINT"{YEL}    {CMH}{CMP} {CMH}{CMM} {
CMG}  {CMH}{CMM} {BLK}{SHL}{CMP} {SHL}{C
MP} {CMG}{CMM} {SHL}{CMP} {SHL}{SH@}{CM5
} {CMM}{CMN}{CMN} {CM+}{CM+}{CM+}
16 PRINT"{YEL}    {SHL}{SH@} {SHL}{SH@} {
SHL}{CMP} {SHL}{SHN} {BLK}{CMG}  {SHL}{C
MP} {SHM}{SHN} {SHL}{CMP} {CMH}{SHM}{CM5
} {CMM}{CMN}{CMN} {CM+}{CM+}{CM+}
17 PRINT"{BLK}   {SHU}{SH*}{SH*}{SH*}{SH*
}{SH*}{SH*}{SH*}{SH*}{SH*}{SH*}{SH*}{SH*
}{SH*}{SH*}{SH*}{SHI} {CM5}  {CM+}{CM+}{
CM+}     {CMM}{CMN}{CMN} {CM+}{CM+}{CM+}
18 PRINT"{BLK}   {SH-}    {CM8}[C] 1984
  {BLK}{SH-}{CM5}   {CM+}{CM+}{CM+}    {
CMM}{CMN}{CMN} {CM+}{CM+}{CM+}
19 PRINT"{BLK}   {SH-}        {CM8}BY
  {BLK}{SH-}{CM5}   {CM+}{CM+}{CM+}    {
CMM}{CMN}{CMN} {CM+}{CM+}{CM+}
20 PRINT"{BLK}   {SH-}{CM8}JOERG WALKOWIA
K{BLK}{SH-}{CM5}   {CM+}{CM+}{CM+}    {
CMM}{SH@}{SHN} {CM+}{CM+}{CM+}
21 PRINT"{BLK}   {SHJ}{SH*}{SH*}{SH*}{SH*
}{SH*}{SH*}{SH*}{SH*}{SH*}{SH*}{SH*}{SH*
}{SH*}{SH*}{SH*}{SHK} {CM5}  {CM+}{CM+}{
CM+}    {SH } {SHN}{SH*}{SH*}{CM+}{CM+}{
CM+}
22 PRINT" {CM2}       {SHU}{SH*}{SH*}{SH*
}{SH*}{SH*}{SH*}{SH*}{SH*}{SH*}{SH*}{SH*
}{SH*}{SH*}{SH*}{SH*}{SHI}{CM5}{CM+}
  {SHN}    {CM+}{CM+}{CM+}
23 PRINT" {CM2}        {SHU}
  {SHI} {CM5}{CM+}     {SHN}       {CM+}{CM+}{
```

```
CM+}
24 PRINT" {CM2}    {SHU}                     {
SHI} {SHN}{CM5}{CM+}    {SHN}       {CM+}{C
M+}{CM+}
25 PRINT" {CM2}    {SHU}{SH*}{SH*}{SH*}{S
H*}{SH*}{SH*}{SH*}{SH*}{SH*}{SH*}{SH*}{S
H*}{SH*}{SH*}{SHI} {SHN} {CM5}{CM+}
   {SHN}{SH*}{SH*}{SH*}{SH*}{SH*}{SHN}{CM
+}{CM+}{CM+}
26 PRINT" {CM2}    {SHO}                    {S
HP}{SHN}  {CM5}{CM+} {SHN}       {SHN} {CM
+}{CM+}{CM+}
27 PRINT" {CM2}    {SHO}{CMY}{CMY}{CMY}{C
MY}{CMY}{CMY}{CMY}{RVS}{YEL} {OFF}{CM2}{
CMY}{CMY}{CMY}{CMY}{CMY}{CMY}{CMY}{SHP}
   {CMH}{CM5}{SHN}       {SHN}
28 PRINT"{CM2}      {CMH}           {RVS}{YEL}
{SHZ}{OFF}{CM2}      {CMM}    {CMH}
29 PRINT"{CM2}      {CMH}                    {C
MM}  {SHN}
30 PRINT"{CM2}     {CMH}                    {C
MM}  {SHN}
31 PRINT"{CM2}     {SHL}{CMP}{CMP}{CMP}{C
MP}{CMP}{CMP}{CMP}{CMP}{CMP}{CMP}{CMP}{C
MP}{CMP}{CMP}{CMP}{SH@}{SHN}
32 PRINT"{ DN}            {CM8}FROM THE {W
HT}ABACUS {CM8}BOOK{ DN}"
33 PRINT"     'ADVENTURE GAMEWRITER'S HAN
DBOOK'"
99 FOR I=1 TO 10000:NEXT
100 REM ------------------------ CHAR
ACTERISTICS
101 :
110 AR=31
120 AO=44
130 AV=11
140 WL=3 : AM=10
150 SP=1
160 AF=7
170 WM=60
171 WE=0
180 ZU=0
185 IM=4 : REM MAXIMUM LOAD TO BE CARRIE
D
186 LM=0 :LI=-1:LW=1:L1=20
190 DIMRA$[AR],DU[AR,6],OB$[AO], RN$[AO]
, OB[AO],FL[AF],MS$[AM],VE$[AV]
199 :
200 REM ------------------------ VERBS
```

```
201 DATA EXAMINE
202 DATA TAKE
203 DATA DROP
204 DATA OPEN
205 DATA USE
206 DATA BREAK
207 DATA LIGHT
208 DATA FILL
209 DATA ENTER
210 DATA EXTINGUISH
211 DATA SECURE
299 :
300 REM --------------------- OBJECTS 2
09
301 DATA"A LOT OF BIG TREES","TREES",1
302 DATA"A LOT OF BIG TREES","TREES",2
303 DATA"SOME BOULDERS","BOULDER",2
304 DATA"A RAMSHACKLE WOODEN HUT","HUT",
3
305 DATA"A DIRTY JAR","JAR",0
306 DATA"HONEY","HONEY",0
307 DATA"A WOODEN BOX","BOX",3
308 DATA"A RICKETY SHELF","SHELF",0
309 DATA"SOME EXPLOSIVES","EXPLOSIVES",0
310 DATA"A MURKY HOLE IN THE GROUND","HO
LE",0
311 DATA"A RUSTY IRON CHEST","CHEST",0
312 DATA"*SILVER COINS*","COINS",0
313 DATA"A DARK CAVE","CAVE",5
314 DATA"A FEROCIOUS LOOKING BEAR","BEAR
",0
315 DATA"NUMEROUS SMALL BUSHES","BUSHES"
,4
316 DATA"SEVERAL IRON BARS","BAR",6
317 DATA"*NUGGETS*","NUGGETS",5
318 DATA"AN IRON BAR","BAR",0
319 DATA A COAL CAR,CAR,7
320 DATA BROKEN DOWN RAILS,RAILS,7
321 DATA A ROPE,ROPE,0
322 DATA A HEAVY PICKAXE,PICKAXE,8
323 DATA AN OLD LANTERN,LANTERN,8
324 DATA THE END OF THE TUNNEL,TUNNEL,9
325 DATA AND IRON HOOK,HOOK,0
326 DATA A SHAFT,SHAFT,9
327 DATA A WOODEN WALL,WALL,10
328 DATA MINERS RUBBLE,RUBBLE,11
329 DATA OLD SACKS,SACKS,0
330 DATA DAMP STONE WALLS,WALL,13
331 DATA AN EVIL SMELLING LIQUID,LIQUID,
```

```
17
332 DATA A CORPSE,CORPSE,18
333 DATA *LUMPS OF SILVER*,SILVER,0
334 DATA *GOLD COINS*,COINS,0
335 DATA COBWEBS,COBWEBS,20
336 DATA A GOLDEN WALL,WALL,22
337 DATA A NOTICE BOARD,BOARD,22
338 DATA *GOLD*,GOLD,31
339 DATA A SEA SHORE,SHORE,30
340 DATA THE LAKE,LAKE,30
341 DATA GOLDEN STONES,STONES,0
342 DATA FUSE,FUSE,0
343 DATA A MATCH,MATCH,-1
344 DATA -,PARADISE,0
499 :
500 REM ------------ SPACE DESCRIPTIONS
501 DATA"IN THE WOOD.",1,1,1,2,0,0
502 DATA"IN THE WOOD.",2,1,1,3,0,0
503 DATA"IN THE WOOD BY AN OVERHANGING R
OCK.",0,4,2,0,0,0
504 DATA"IN A CLEARING IN THE FOREST.",3
,0,5,0,0,0
505 DATA"IN A CLEARING BY A HILLSIDE.",0
,0,6,4,0,0
506 DATA"BY THE ENTRANCE TO AN OLD MINE.
",7,0,1,5,0,0
507 DATA IN THE ENTRANCE.,8,6,0,0,0,0
508 DATA IN A RECESS OF THE TUNNEL.,9,7,
8,10,0,0
509 DATA AT THE END OF THE TUNNEL.,0,8,0
,0,0,0
510 DATA IN A SIDE-TUNNEL.,11,0,8,0,0,0
511 DATA BY AND OLD DEMOLITION SITE.,0,1
0,0,0,0,0
512 DATA IN THE CAVE.,0,5,0,13,0,0
513 DATA IN THE CAVE.,0,0,12,14,0,0
514 DATA IN THE CAVE.,0,16,13,15,0,0
515 DATA IN THE CAVE.,0,0,14,0,0,0
516 DATA ON A PATH.,14,0,0,17,0,0
517 DATA IN A SIDE CAVE.,0,0,16,0,0,0
518 DATA ON THE FOOR OF THE SHAFT.,0,0,1
9,0,0,0
519 DATA ON A WINDING PATH.,24,0,20,18,0
,0
520 DATA IN A WIDE CORRIDOR.,0,0,21,19,0
,0
521 DATA ON OLD DEMOLITION SITE,22,11,11
,20,11,0
522 DATA IN THE DOME OF A CAVE.,0,21,0,0
```

```
,27,0
523 DATA IN AN UNDERGROUND PARADISE.,0,0
,0,0,0,0
524 DATA ON A WINDING PATH.,26,19,24,24,
24,24
525 DATA ON A WINDING PATH.,27,24,24,29,
26,24
526 DATA ON A WINDING PATH.,27,24,26,27,
27,24
527 DATA ON A WINDING PATH.,25,24,26,27,
26,24
528 DATA ON A WINDING PATH.,24,26,26,27,
0,0
529 DATA ON A WINDING PATH.,0,27,30,27,0
,0
530 DATA BY AN UNDERGROUND LAKE.,28,0,0,
0,0,0
531 DATA IN A SMALL CAVE.,30,0,0,0,0,0
599 :
600 REM ------------------- INFORMATION
601 MS$(1)="I CAN'T SEE ANYTHING SPECIAL
."
602 MS$(2)="I AM NOT THAT STRONG."
603 MS$(3)="WHAT DO YOU MEAN ?"
604 MS$(4)="THE BEAR TAKES THE HONEY AND
"
605 MS$(5)="DISAPPEARS INTO THE DEPTHS O
F THE CAVE."
606 MS$(6)="HOW CAN I BREAK THE CHAIN ?"
607 MS$(7)="THE ROPES STILL HANGING FROM
 IT"
608 MS$(8)="THAT IT WAS PULLED ALONG WIT
H."
609 MS$(9)="WHEN GREED TAKES OVER, DEATH
 IS NOT FAR BEHIND."
698 :
699 REM ------------- 2, TITLE: INTRODUC
TION
700 PRINT"{CLR}":POKE53280,0:POKE53281,0
:PRINT"{PUR}";CHR$(14);
710 PRINT"{SHW}ELCOME TO THE ADVENTURE..
."
715 PRINTSPC(15)"{ DN}{YEL}{SHG}{SHO}{SH
L}{SHD}{SHR}{SHU}{SHS}{SHH}{ DN}"
720 PRINT"{WHT}{SH*}{SH*}{SH*}{SH*}{SH*}
{SH*}{SH*}{SH*}{SH*}{SH*}{SH*}{SH*}
{SH*}{SH*}{SH*}{SH*}{SH*}{SH*}{SH*}
{SH*}{SH*}{SH*}{SH*}{SH*}{SH*}{SH*}
{SH*}{SH*}{SH*}{SH*}{SH*}{SH*}{SH*}{SH*}
```

```
{SH*}{SH*}"
725 PRINT"{SHS}OME DAYS AGO WHILE LOOKIN
G FOR A   "
730 PRINT"FORTUNE IN THE NEW WORLD,YOU M
ET A "
735 PRINT"CRITICALLY ILL OLD MAN TO WHOM
 YOU GAVE"
740 PRINT"HELP IN HIS LAST HOURS.    "
745 PRINT"{SHO}UT OF GRATITUDE HE TOLD Y
OU ABOUT"
750 PRINT"HIS GOLDMINE AND THE REST OF H
IS "
755 PRINT"WEALTH HIDDEN THERE."
760 PRINT"{SHM}ANY DANGERS FACED YOU ON
THE WAY THERE,";
765 PRINT"SOON YOU WILL HAVE REACHED YOU
R GOAL"
770 PRINT"AND IT WILL BE SEEN WHETHER TH
E OLD MAN"
775 PRINT"WAS SPEAKING THE TRUTH OR HAD
MADE IT"
780 PRINT"ALL UP."
785 PRINT
790 PRINT"{SH*}{SH*}{SH*}{SH*}{SH*}{SH*}
{SH*}{SH*}{SH*}{SH*}{SH*}{SH*}{SH*}{SH*}
{SH*}{SH*}{SH*}{SH*}{SH*}{SH*}{SH*}{SH*}
{SH*}{SH*}{SH*}{SH*}{SH*}{SH*}{SH*}{SH*}
{SH*}{SH*}{SH*}{SH*}{SH*}{SH*}{SH*}{SH*}
"
799 :
800 REM -------------- READ PLAYING DAT
A IN
810 FOR I=1 TO AV
815 READ VERB$[I]:VERB$[I]=LEFT$[VERB$[I
],WL]
820 NEXT I
830 FOR OB=1 TO AO
835 READ OB$[OB], RN$[OB], OB[OB]:RN$[OB
]=LEFT$[RN$[OB],WL]
840 NEXT OB
845 FOR RA=1 TO AR
850 READ RA$[RA]
855 FOR RI=1 TO 6
860 READ DU[RA,RI]
865 NEXT RI
870 NEXT RA
875 :
880 PRINT"{ DN}          DO YOU WANT ADVIC
E FOR"
```

```
885 INPUT"          WHAT TO DO NEXT ";EI$
890 IF EI$="Y" THEN GOSUB 900
895 GOTO 1000
899 :
900 REM -------- 3, TITLE: INSTRUCTIONS
910 PRINT"{CLR}";CHR$[14];
920 PRINT"  -64 - {SHA}DVENTURE {SHS}YST
EM, {SHV}ERSION 1.0"
930 PRINT"         [C] 1984  BY {SHW}ALKO
WIAK"
940 PRINT"-----------------------------
---------"
950 PRINT"{SHI}MAGINE A ROBOT WHOM YOU C
AN CONTROL"
951 PRINT"WITH A LOT OF COMMANDS. {SHI}
AM THAT ROBOT"
952 PRINT"AND ON YOUR BEHALF SHALL EXPOS
E MYSELF"
953 PRINT"TO THE DANGERS OF THE BOLDEST
OF "
954 PRINT"ADVENTURES."
955 PRINT"{SHT}O ENABLE YOU TO MAKE ME A
CT SENSIBLY,"
956 PRINT"{SHI} SHALL ACCURATELY DESCRIB
E THE"
957 PRINT"SITUATION IN WHICH I HAPPEN TO
 FIND "
958 PRINT"MYSELF AT ANY GIVEN TIME. {SHW
}HEN YOU"
959 PRINT"TELL ME IN TWO WORDS SUCH AS,
          "
960 PRINT"{SHE}{SHX}{SHA}{SHM}{SHI}{SHN}
{SHE} {SHD}{SHO}{SHO}{SHR}, WHAT {SHI} S
HOULD DO."
961 PRINT"APART FROM THAT I UNDERSTAND T
HE WORDS"
962 PRINT"         {SHI}{SHN}{SHV}ENTORY
  {SHS}{SHA}{SHV}{SHE} {SHL}{SHO}{SHA}{S
HD} "
963 PRINT"         {SHV}{SHO}{SHC}ABULAR
Y {SHH}{SHE}{SHL}{SHP} {SHE}{SHN}{SHD}
"
964 PRINT"        {SHS}{SHC}{SHO}RE    AND
   {SHI}{SHN}{SHS}TRUCTIONS "
975 PRINT"-----------------------------
--------"
980 PRINT"{ DN}{ DN}"SPC[11]"[{SHP}RESS
A KEY]";
985 GET EI$: IF EI$="" THEN 985
```

```
990 PRINT"{CLR}":PRINTCHR$[142]:RETURN
995 :
999 REM --------- BEGINNING ADVENTURE-DR
IVER
1000 PRINT"{CLR}":PRINTCHR$[142]
1010 LE$="
          "
1020 DATA NORTH, SOUTH, WEST, EAST, UP,
DOWN
1030 FOR RI=1 TO 6
1040 READ RI$[RI]
1050 NEXT RI
1070 PRINT"{CLR}":POKE 53280,0:POKE 5328
1,0:PRINT"{CM7}"
1080 ZU=ZU+1 : LW=LW+1 : REM BEGINNING N
EW MOVE
1084 IF LW=LM THEN GOSUB 3000
1085 IF WE=WM THEN GOTO 4800
1090 POKE211,0:POKE214,0:SYS 58732
1100 FOR ZE=1 TO 10
1110 PRINT LE$
1120 NEXT ZE
1130 POKE211,0:POKE214,0:SYS 58732
1131 REM --------------------- NO LIGH
T
1132 IF LI=-1 THEN 1140
1133 PRINT"I DON'T QUITE KNOW WHERE I AM
."
1134 PRINT"IT'S TOO DARK TO SEE ANYTHING
."
1135 PRINT"{ DN}I CAN'T SEE THE EXITS EI
THER NOW.":GOTO1330
1140 PRINT"I AM{SH }";
1150 PRINTRA$[SP]
1160 PRINT"I CAN SEE ";:GE=0
1170 FOR I=1 TO AO
1180 IF OB[I]<>SPTHEN 1210
1190 IF POS[O]+LEN[OB$[I]]+2<39 THEN PRI
NT OB$[I];", ";:GE=-1:GOTO 1210
1200 IF POS[O]+LEN[OB$[I]]+2>=39 THEN PR
INT : GOTO 1190
1210 NEXT I:IF NOT GE THEN PRINT"NOTHING
 IN PARTICULAR"
1220 PRINT"{LFT}{LFT}."
1230 PRINT LE$
1240 PRINT "{CM1}I CAN GO ";
1250 FOR RI=1 TO 6
1260 IF DU[SP,RI]=0 THEN GOTO 1310
1270 IF POS[O]=14 THEN PRINT RI$[RI];:GO
```

```
TO 1310
1280 IFPOS(0)+LEN(RI$(RI))<37 THENPRINT"
, ";RI$(RI);:GOTO 1310
1290 IFPOS(0)+LEN(RI$(RI))>=37 THEN PRIN
T",":PRINT RI$(RI);:GOTO1310
1300 IF POS(0)<16 AND POS(0)>2 THEN PRIN
T", ";RI$(RI);:GOTO 1310
1310 NEXT RI
1320 PRINT"."
1330 PRINT"{WHT}{SH*}{SH*}{SH*}{SH*}{SH*
}{SH*}{SH*}{SH*}{SH*}{SH*}{SH*}{SH*}{SH*
}{SH*}{SH*}{SH*}{SH*}{SH*}{SH*}{SH*}{SH*
}{SH*}{SH*}{SH*}{SH*}{SH*}{SH*}{SH*}{SH*
}{SH*}{SH*}{SH*}{SH*}{SH*}{SH*}{SH*}{SH*
}{SH*}{SH*}"
1340 IF WE=IM THEN GOTO 4800
1350 IF SP=15 THEN MS$(0)="THE BEAR IS T
HERE.":FORI=1TO1000:NEXT:GOTO4500
1360 IF LW<=0 THEN LI=0
1370 IFEX=ZU AND SP=20THENMS$(0)="OUCH!-
NOW IT'S SCRATCHED ME.":GOTO4500
1380 IF SP>18 AND OB(23)<>-1 THEN LI=0
1390 POKE 211,0:POKE 214,24:SYS 58732:PR
INT"{WHT}";:INPUT"WHAT SHALL I DO";EI$:P
RINT"{CM8}";
1395 RL=LM-LW:IF (RL>0ANDRL<15)THEN PRIN
T"IN";LM-LW;"MOVES YOU WILL BE IN DARKNE
SS"
1400 IF LEN(EI$)>2 THEN 1500
1410 IFEI$="N"ANDDU(SP,1)<>0THENSP=DU(SP
,1):PRINT"O.K.":GOTO1080
1420 IFEI$="S"ANDDU(SP,2)<>0THENSP=DU(SP
,2):PRINT"O.K.":GOTO1080
1430 IFEI$="W"ANDDU(SP,3)<>0THENSP=DU(SP
,3):PRINT"O.K.":GOTO1080
1440 IFEI$="E"ANDDU(SP,4)<>0THENSP=DU(SP
,4):PRINT"O.K.":GOTO1080
1450 IFEI$="U"ANDDU(SP,5)<>0THENSP=DU(SP
I,5):PRINT"O.K.":GOTO1080
1460 IFEI$="D"ANDDU(SP,6)<>0THENSP=DU(SP
,6):PRINT"O.K.":GOTO1080
1470 PRINT"THAT DOESN'T LEAD ANYWHERE !"
:GOTO 1080
1490 IF LEN(EI$)>6 THEN GOTO 2000
1498 :
1499 REM ------------ START INVENTORY --
-------
1500 IF LEFT$(EI$,3)<>"INV" THEN GOTO 15
60
```

```
1510 PRINT"I AM CARRYING THE FOLLOWING:"
1520 FOR I=1 TO AO
1530 IF OB[I]=-1 THEN PRINT OB$[I]
1540 NEXT I
1550 GOTO 1080
1551 REM ------------- END INVENTORY ---
--------
1559 REM ----------------------------
 SCORE LIST170
1560 IF LEFT$[EI$,3]<>"SCO" THEN GOTO 16
00
1561 PRINT"OUT OF";WM;"POINTS YOU HAVE,I
N";ZU;"MOVES,"
1562 PRINT "GAINED";WE;"POINTS! WHICH CO
RRESPONDS TO"
1563 PRINT"A SCORE OF";WE/ZU;"POINTS."
1565 GOTO 1080
1599 REM ------------------------- SAV
E GAME
1600 IF LEFT$[EI$,4]<>"SAVE" THEN GOTO 1
700
1605 PRINT"{CLR}"SPC[10];:INPUT"{ DN}{ D
N}ENTER NAME";EI$
1610 IF LEN[EI$]>16 THEN 1605
1615 PRINT"{ DN}{ DN}SAVING ";EI$
1620 OPEN 2,8,2,"@0:"+EI$+",S,W"
1625 PRINT#2,SP
1627 PRINT#2,WE:PRINT#2,L1:PRINT#2,LM:PR
INT#2,LW
1628 PRINT#2, ZU
1630 FOR I=1 TO AO
1631 PRINT#2,OB[I]
1632 NEXT I
1633 PRINT"."
1635 FOR RA=1 TO AR
1636 FOR RI=1 TO 6
1637 PRINT#2, DU[RA,RI]
1638 NEXT RI
1639 NEXT RA
1640 PRINT".";
1645 FOR I=1 TO AF
1646 PRINT#2,FL[I]
1647 NEXT I
1648 PRINT".";
1650 CLOSE 2
1660 GOSUB 1680
1670 PRINT"{CLR}":GOTO 1080
1678 :
1679 REM -------------------- DISK ERROR
```

```
1680 OPEN1,8,15
1681 INPUT#1,A,B$,C,D
1682 IFA<>OTHENPRINT:PRINT"{ DN}{ DN}{RV
S}{RED}ERROR: ":PRINTB$:FORI=1TO 5000:NE
XT:CLOSE2
1683 CLOSE1
1684 RETURN :REM ------------ END
1698 :
1699 REM ---------------------- LOAD GAM
E
1700 IF LEFT$(EI$,4)<>"LOAD" THEN GOTO 1
800
1705 PRINT"{CLR}"SPC[10]"LOAD GAME":INPU
T"{ DN}{ DN}WHAT IS THE GAME'S NAME";EI$
1710 IF LEN[EI$]>16 THEN 1805
1715 PRINT"{ DN}{ DN}LOADING "EI$" ";
1720 OPEN 2,8,2,EI$+",S,R"
1725 INPUT#2,SP
1726 PRINT".";
1727 INPUT#2, WE:INPUT#2,L1:INPUT#2,LM:I
NPUT#2,LW
1728 INPUT#2, ZU
1730 FOR I=1 TO AO
1731 INPUT#2,OB[I]
1732 NEXT I
1733 PRINT".";
1735 FOR RA=1 TO AR
1736 FOR RI=1 TO 6
1737 INPUT#2, DU[RA,RI]
1738 NEXT RI
1739 NEXT RA
1740 PRINT".";
1745 FOR I=1 TO AF
1746 INPUT#2,FL[I]
1747 NEXT I
1748 PRINT".";
1750 CLOSE 2
1760 GOSUB 1680
1770 PRINT"{CLR}":GOTO 1080
1771 REM ------------------ END OF LOAD G
AME
1778 :
1798 :
1799 REM ---------------------- VOCABULAR
Y
1800 IF LEFT$(EI$,3)<>"VOC" THEN GOTO 19
00
1805 PRINT"{CLR}":PRINT"{YEL}I UNDERSTAN
D THE FOLLOWING VERBS:{ DN}{ DN}"
```

```
1806 RESTORE
1810 FOR I=1 TO AV
1820 READ VO$:PRINT VO$
1830 NEXT I
1840 GOSUB 1890
1845 PRINT"{CLR}":PRINT"AND HERE AR THE
OBJECTS THAT I KNOW:{ DN}"
1849 ZE=0
1850 FOR I=1 TO AO
1855 ZE=ZE+1
1860 READ VO$,VO$,X:PRINTVO$
1865 IF ZE=20 THEN GOSUB 1890
1866 IF ZE=20 THEN ZE=1 : PRINT"{CLR}"
1870 NEXT I
1880 GOSUB 1890:PRINT"{CLR}":GOTO 1080
1890 PRINTSPC[24]"{ DN}PRESS SPACE BAR";
1895 GETEI$:IFEI$=""THEN 1895
1896 PRINT"{CLR}":RETURN
1900 IF LEFT$[EI$,3]<>"INS" THEN GOTO 19
50
1910 GOSUB 900
1920 GOTO 1080
1950 IF LEFT$[EI$,3]<>"END" THEN GOTO 19
60
1955 PRINT"{CLR}THE AUTHOR WISHES YOU BE
TTER LUCK TIME.{ DN}{ DN}{ DN}{ DN}{ DN}
":END
1959 REM ------------------------ HELPR
EADY
1960 IF LEFT$[EI$,4]<>"HELP" THEN GOTO 2
000
1970 IFSP=4 AND OB[10]=OTHEN PRINT "I NE
ARLY FELL DOWN A HOLE.":GOTO1080
1971 IF SP=4 AND OB[11]=SP AND NOTFL[2]
THEN PRINTMS$[6]:GOTO1080
1975 PRINT"YOU SHOULD LOOK BEFORE YOU LE
AP":GOTO 1080
1979 REM -------------------- END HELP
1990 :
1999 REM -------------- ANALYSE THE INPU
T
2000 LN=LEN[EI$]
2010 FOR EL=1 TO LN
2020 TEST$=MID$[EI$,EL,1]
2030 IF TEST$<>" "THEN NEXT EL
2040 EV$=LEFT$[EI$,WL]
2050 RL=LN-EL
2060 IF RL<0 THEN 2090
2070 EO$=RIGHT$[EI$,RL]
```

```
2080 EO$=LEFT$(EO$,WL)
2090 FOR VN=1 TO AV
2100 IF EV$=VERB$(VN) THEN 2130
2110 NEXT VN
2120 PRINT"I DON'T UNDERSTAND THAT VERB!
":GOTO 1080
2130 FOR N=1 TO AO
2140 IF EO$=RN$(N) THEN 2200
2150 NEXT N
2160 PRINT"I DON'T KNOW THAT OBJECT!":GO
TO 1080
2169 :
2170 REM
2180 REM  EXAMINE  , TAKE,DROP, OPEN  ,
 USE ,DESTROY  , LIGHT , FILL
2200 ON VN GOTO 5000,2210,7000,8000,9000
,10000,11000,12000,13000,14000,15000
2201 :
2210 AN=0
2220 FOR I=1 TO AO
2230 IF OB(I)=-1 THEN AN=AN+1
2240 IF AN=IM THEN PRINT"I CAN'T CARRY A
NYMORE !":GOTO1080
2250 NEXT I
2260 GOTO 6000
2270 REM ------ END OF ROOM TEST
2999 REM -------------- LIGHT SWITCH
3000 IF LI=-1 THEN LI=0
3010 IF LI=0 THEN LI=-1
3020 LW=0
3030 RETURN
3040 REM ----------- END OF LIGHT SECTIO
N
4498 :
4499 REM ------------------- END OF GAM
E
4500 PRINT"{CLR}":REM ------- PLAYER DEA
D -----
4600 PRINT "THIS IS THE END!":PRINT:PRIN
TMS$(O)
4610 PRINT"{ DN}{ DN}{ DN}I AM DEAD  !":
PRINT
4620 INPUT"SHALL I TRY AGAIN ";EI$
4630 IF LEFT$(EI$,1)="Y"THEN RUN
4640 PRINT"{CLR}":END
4641 :
4799 :
4800 PRINT"{CLR}":REM ----- PLAYER WINS
  -
```

```
4805 EW=WE/ZU
4810 PRINT"WELL DONE !"
4815 PRINT"YOU HAVE SOLVED THE ADVENTURE
."
4820 PRINT
4825 PRINT"IN";ZU;"MOVES YOU HAVE SCORED
"
4830 PRINT EW;"POINTS."
4835 PRINT"YOU HAVE GOT A ";
4840 IF EW<.5 THEN MS$[0]="ROTTEN"
4845 IF EW>.5 THEN MS$[0]="AVERAGE"
4850 IF EW>1.0 THEN MS$[0]="GOOD"
4855 IF EW>1.5 THEN MS$[0]="VERY GOOD"
4860 PRINTMS$[0];" SCORE."
4865 PRINT
4899 END
4998 :
4999 REM -------------- EXECUTE PLAYERS
MOVE
5000 IF OB[N]<>SP AND OB[N]<>-1 THEN GOT
O 5900 : REM EXAMINE
5002 IF N=1 THEN PRINTMS$[1]:GOTO1080
5003 IF N=3 THEN PRINTMS$[1]:GOTO1080
5004 IF N=4 THEN PRINT"IN THE CORNER IS
A SHELF.":OB[8]=SP:GOTO1080
5005 IF N=5 AND NOTFL[3] THEN PRINT "THE
 JAR IS FULL OF HONEY.":GOTO1080
5006 IF N=6 THEN PRINTMS$[1]:GOTO1080
5007 IF N=7 ANDOB[9]=0THENPRINT"THE BOX
HAS EXPLOSIVES IN IT.":GOTO1080
5008 IFN=8 AND OB[5]=0THEN PRINT"THERE I
S A JAR ON THE SHELF.":OB[5]=SP:GOTO1080
5009 IF N=8 AND OB[5]<>0 THEN PRINT MS$[
1]:GOTO1080
5010 IF N=10THEN PRINT"THERE IS AN IRON
CHEST IN THE HOLE.":OB[11]=SP:GOTO1080
5011 IFN=11ANDNOTFL[1] THEN PRINT"IT IS
LOCKED WITH AN IRON CHAIN.":GOTO1080
5012 IFN=11ANDFL[1]ANDNOTFL[2]THENPRINT"
I CAN'T SEE ANYTHING FROM OUTSIDE.":GOTO
1080
5013 IF N=11ANDFL[1]ANDFL[2]THENPRINT"IT
'S FULL OF SILVER COINS.":OB[12]=SP:GOTO
1080
5014 IF N=12 THEN PRINT"THAT'S JUST WHAT
 I'M LOOKING FOR!":GOTO1080
5015 IFN=13THENPRINT"I HAVE DISTURBED A
BEAR.":OB[14]=SP:GOTO1080
5017 IFN=15THENPRINT"IN THE BUSHES IS A
```

```
HOLE.":OB[10]=SP:GOTO1080
5018 IF N=16 THEN PRINT"THEY LOOK VERY S
TRONG.":GOTO1080
5019 IF N=17 THEN PRINT"IT IS PURE GOLD
!":GOTO1080
5020 IF N=19 AND OB[21]=0 THEN PRINTMS$[
7]:PRINTMS$[8]:OB[21]=SP:GOTO1080
5021 IF N=23 THEN PRINT"IT IS AN OLD OIL
 LAMP.":GOTO1080
5022 IF N=24 THEN PRINT"THERE IS A HOOK
IN THE WALL.":OB[25]=SP:GOTO1080
5023 IF N=25 THEN PRINT"I CAN'T IT'S STU
CK.":GOTO1080
5024 IF N=26THENMS$[0]="IT IS VERY DEEP
- AND I WAS TOO NEAR THE EDGE.":GOTO4500
5025 IF N=27 THEN PRINT"THAT CARPENTER W
AS A REAL EXPERT":GOTO1080
5026 IF N=28 AND OB[N]=0THEN PRINT"I CAN
 SEE TWO SACKS.":OB[29]=SP:GOTO1080
5027 IF N=29 THEN PRINT"THEY ARE FULL OF
 GOLD DUST.":GOTO1080
5028 IF N=31 THEN PRINT"IT'S OILY AND ST
ICKS TO YOUR HANDS.":GOTO1080
5029 IFN=32THENPRINT"IT STINKS !"
5030 IFN=32ANDOB[34]=0THENPRINT"THERE AR
E GOLD COINS IN THE POCKET.":OB[34]=SP:G
OTO1080
5031 IF N=35 THEN PRINT"THERE AREN'T ANY
 COBWEBS AT ALL.":OB[N]=0:OB[42]=SP
5032 IF N=35 THEN PRINT"IT IS A FUSE.":G
OTO1080
5033 IF N=36 THEN PRINT"IT REALLY IS PUR
E GOLD.":GOTO1080
5034 IF N=37 THEN PRINT"IT SAYS ON IT":P
RINTMS$[9]:GOTO1080
5035 IF N=42 THEN PRINT"IT LEADS UP TO T
HE CEILING.":GOTO1080
5036 IF N=43 THEN PRINT"IT IS AN ORDINAR
Y MATCH."
5037 IFN=32ANDFL[4]ANDOB[33]<>-2THENPRIN
T"IT IS ON SOME SILVER.":OB[33]=SP :GOTO
1080
5899 PRINTMS$[1]:GOTO1080
5900 REM  OBJECT NOT HERE
5901 IF N=1 AND SP=2 THEN PRINTMS$[1]:GO
TO1080
5902 IFN=6 AND OB[5]=-1 THEN PRINT"IT IS
 SWEET AND GOOD.":GOTO1080
5903 IF N=6 AND OB[5]<>-1 THEN PRINT"I H
```

```
AVEN'T ANY HONEY !":GOTO1080
5904 IFN=9ANDOB[7]=SPOR OB[7]=-1THENPRIN
T"IT LOOKS LIKE IT WILL BLOW UP!":GOTO10
80
5905 IF M=9 THEN PRINT"THE EXPLOSIVE LOO
KS DANGEROUS !":GOTO1080
5910 IFN=1ANDSP=5ANDOB[14]=5THENPRINT"I
SEEM TO WHET HIS APPETITE !":GOTO1080
5911 IF N=20 AND SP=22 THENPRINTMS$[9]:G
OTO1080
5912 IF N=44 AND SP=23 THEN MS$[0]="I AM
 IN THE KINGDOM OF THE DEAD.":GOTO4500
5990 PRINT "THERE IS NOTHING LIKE THAT H
ERE.":GOTO 1080
6000 IF OB[N]<>SP AND OB[N]<>-1 THEN GOT
O 6900
6001 IF N=1 THEN PRINT MS$[2]:GOTO 1080
6002 IF N=3 THEN PRINT MS$[2]:GOTO 1080
6003 IF N=4 THEN PRINT MS$[3]:GOTO 1080
6004 IF N=8 THEN PRINT MS$[2]:GOTO 1080
6005 IF N=11THENPRINT MS$[2]:GOTO 1080
6006 IF N=10THEN PRINT MS$[3]:GOTO 1080
6007 IF N=13THEN PRINT MS$[3]:GOTO 1080
6008 IF N=15THEN PRINT MS$[2]:GOTO 1080
6010 IF N=5 THEN OB[5]=-1:PRINT"O.K.":GO
TO1080
6011 IF N=6 THEN OB[5]=-1:PRINT"O.K.":GO
TO1080
6012 IF N=7 THEN OB[7]=-1:PRINT"O.K.":GO
TO1080
6014 IF N=12 AND OB[N]=4 THEN PRINT"O.K.
":OB[12]=-2:RN$[12]=" ":WE=WE+10:GOTO108
0
6015 IF N=1 AND SP=5 THEN MS$[0]="THE BE
AR HAS KILLED ME.":GOTO4500
6016 IF N=16 THEN PRINT"O.K.":OB[18]=-1:
GOTO1080
6017 IFN=17ANDOB[N]=5ANDFL[3]THENPRINT"O
.K.":OB[17]=-2:RN$[N]=" ":WE=WE+10:GOTO1
080
6018 IF N=17 AND NOT FL[3] THEN MS$[0]="
THE BEAR IS ATTACKING ME.":GOTO4500
6019 IF N=12 AND OB[N]=-1 THEN PRINT"NOW
 I'VE GOT THE SILVER !":GOTO1080
6020 IF N=17 AND OB[N]=-1 THEN PRINT"NOW
 I'VE GOT THE GOLD !":GOTO1080
6021 IF N=19 THEN PRINTMS$[2]:GOTO1080
6022 IF N=21 AND FL[4] THEN PRINT"O.K.":
OB[N]=-1:GOTO1080
```

```
6023 IF N=22 THEN PRINT"O.K.":OB[N]=-1:G
OTO1080
6024 IF N=24 THEN PRINT"O.K.":OB[N]=-1:G
OTO1080
6025 IF N=25 THEN PRINT"IT'S TOO FAR IN
THE ROCK.":GOTO1080
6026 IF N=27 THEN PRINTMS$[3]:GOTO1080
6027 IF N=28 THEN PRINT"AND WHAT SHALL I
 DO WITH IT?":GOTO1080
6030 IFN=31ANDOB[5]<>-1THENPRINT"WITH WH
AT ?":GOTO1080
6031 IFN=31ANDOB[5]=-1THENPRINT"O.K. - T
HE JAR IS FULL.":FL[6]=-1:GOTO1080
6032 IF N=32THENPRINT"O.K. - OH, WHAT IS
 THAT ?":FL[5]=-1:GOTO1080
6033 IF N=33 AND OB[N]=SP THEN PRINT"O.K
.":OB[N]=-2:RN$[N]=" ":WE=WE+10:GOTO1080
6034 IF N=34 AND OB[N]=SP THEN PRINT"O.K
.":OB[N]=-2:WE=WE+10:RN$[N]=" ":GOTO1080
6035 IFN=35THENPRINT"THERE AREN'T ANY CO
BWEBS AT ALL, IT WAS"
6036 IFN=35THENPRINT"A FUSE.":OB[N]=0:OB
[42]=-1:GOTO1080
6037 IF N=37 THEN OB[N]=-1:PRINT"O.K.":G
OTO1080
6038 IF N=41 THEN OB[N]=-1:PRINT"O.K.":G
OTO1080
6039 IF N=42 THEN OB[N]=-1:PRINT"O.K.":G
OTO1080
6041 IF N=21 AND NOT FL[4] THEN PRINT"IT
 IS FASTENED TO THE CAR.":GOTO1080
6042 IF N=23 THEN PRINT"O.K.":OB[N]=-1:G
OTO1080
6043 IF N=29 AND OB[N]=SP THEN PRINT"O.K
.":OB[N]=-2:RN$[N]=" ":WE=WE+10:GOTO1080
6044 IF N=38 AND OB[N]=SP THEN PRINT"O.K
.":OB[N]=-2:RN$[N]=" ":WE=WE+10:GOTO1080
6900 IF N=9THENMS$[0]="THE EXPLOSIVE WHE
N I TOUCHED IT.":GOTO4500
6910 IF N=20 AND SP=22 THENPRINTMS$[9]:G
OTO1080
6998 PRINT "I DON'T UNDERSTAND WHAT YOU
MEAN !":GOTO1080
7000 IF N=16 AND OB[18]=-1 THEN PRINT"O.
K.":OB[18]=SP:GOTO1080
7005 IF OB[N]<>-1 THEN PRINT"BUT I DON'T
 HAVE ANYTHING LIKE THAT.":GOTO1080
7010 IFN=6ANDSP=5THENOB[6]=0:FL[3]=-1:PR
INTMS$[4]:PRINTMS$[5]:OB[14]=15:OB[5]=14
```

```
:GOTO1080
7020 IFN=5ANDSP=5 THENOB[5]=14:FL[3]=-1:
PRINTMS$[4]:PRINTMS$[5]:OB[14]=15:GOTO10
80
7030 IF N=17 THEN OB[N]=SP:WE=WE-10:PRIN
T"O.K.":GOTO1080
7900 OB[N]=SP:PRINT"O.K.":GOTO1080
8000 IF OB[N]<>SP AND OB[N]<>-1 THENPRIN
T"THER'S NOTHING LIKE THAT HERE.":GOTO10
80
8005 IF N=4 AND SP=3 THEN PRINT"THE HUT
WAS OPEN.":GOTO1080
8010 IF N=5 THEN PRINT"O.K.":GOTO1080
8020 IF N=11 AND NOT FL[1] THEN PRINT"A
CHAIN STOPS YOU.":GOTO1080
8025 IF N=11 AND FL[1] THEN PRINT"O.K. -
 THE LID FOLDS BACK.":FL[2]=-1: GOTO1080
8030 IF N=23 THEN PRINT"O.K.":GOTO1080
8035 IF N=29 THEN PRINT"O.K.":GOTO1080
8040 IF N=32 THEN PRINT"I'M SORRY !":PRI
NT"I'M NOT FRANKENSTEIN.":GOTO1080
8045 IF N=36 THEN PRINT"WHAT ?":GOTO1080
8999 PRINT"I DON'T UNDERSTAND WHAT YOU M
EAN.":GOTO1080
9000 IF OB[N]<>SP AND OB[N]<>-1 THEN GOT
O 9900   REM  EXAMINE
9020 IF N=19 THEN PRINT"HOW AND WHY ?":G
OTO1080
9030 IF N=21 THEN PRINT"HOW AND WHY ?":G
OTO1080
9900 IF N=16 AND OB[18]=-1AND SP=4THEN P
RINT"THE CHAIN IS BREAKING.":FL[1]=-1:GO
TO1080
9999 PRINT"I DON'T UNDERSTAND WHAT YOU M
EAN.":GOTO1080
10000 IFN=16ANDSP=4 AND OB[18]THENPRINT"
THE CHAIN IS BREAKING.":FL[1]=-1:GOTO108
0
10010 IF N=19 AND SP=4 AND OB[19]<>-1 TH
EN PRINT"WHAT WITH ?":FL=-1:GOTO1080
10020 IF N=36 AND OB[22]=-1 THEN PRINT"O
.K.":DU[22,1]=23:GOTO1080
10030 IF N=21 AND[OB[N]=SP OR OB[N]=-1]T
HENPRINT"O.K.":FL[4]=-1:GOTO1080
10040 IF N=27 AND OB[22]=-1 THEN PRINT"O
.K.":DU[10,2]=12:GOTO1080
10050 IF N=27 AND OB[22]<>-1 THEN PRINT"
WHAT WITH ?":GOTO1080
10999 PRINT"I DON'T UNDERSTAND WHAT YOU
```

```
MEAN.":GOTO1080
11000 IF OB[43]<>-1 THEN PRINT"I HAVE NO
THING TO LIGHT IT WITH.":GOTO1080
11010 IF N=8 AND LZ<0 THEN PRINT"THERE I
S NO OIL IN THE LAMP !:GOTO1080
11020 IFN=42AND[OB[43]=-1OR LIGHT]THENPR
INT"SSSSSSSSSS":FL[7]=-1:EX=ZU+3:OB[N]=0
11021 IF N=42AND[OB[43]=-1 OR LI]THENDU[
30,2]=31:DU[31,1]=30:GOTO1080
11030 IF N=23AND OB[23]=-1 THENPRINT"O.K
. - THE LAMP IS LIGHT.":LM=L1:LW=1:GOTO1
080
11040 IFN=43 THEN PRINT"O.K. - THE MATCH
 IS GLOWING.":GOTO1080
11998 PRINT"I DON'T UNDERSTAND WHAT YOU
MEAN.":GOTO1080
12000 REM --------------------- ACTION:
FILL
12010 IF N=23AND[FL[6]ANDOB[23]=-1]THENL
M=50:FL[6]=0:LW=0: PRINT"O.K.": GOTO1080
12020 IF N=5 AND SP=17 THEN FL[6]=-1:PRI
NT"THE JAR IS FULL.":GOTO1080
12030 IF N=43 AND OB[43]=-1 THEN PRINT"T
HE MATCH IS GLOWING":GOTO1080
12998 PRINT"I DON'T UNDERSTAND WHAT YOU
MEAN.":GOTO1080
13000 REM --------------------- ACTION:E
NTER
13010 IF N=13 AND SP=5 THEN SP=12:PRINT
"O.K.":GOTO1080
13998 PRINT"I DON'T UNDERSTAND WHAT YOU
MEAN.":GOTO1080
14000 IF N=23 AND OB[N]=-1 THEN L1=LM-LW
:PRINT"O.K.":GOTO1080
14998 PRINT"I DON'T UNDERSTAND WHAT YOU
MEAN.":GOTO1080
15000 IFN=21ANDSP=9THENPRINT"O.K.":OB[N]
=9:DU[9,6]=18:DU[18,5]=9:GOTO1080
15998 PRINT"I DON'T UNDERSTAND WHAT YOU
MEAN.":GOTO1080

READY.
```

```
3 REM  THE ENCHANTED CASTLE
4 REM  [C] 1984 BY J.WALKOWIAK
8 REM"--------------------------------
----
10 PRINT"{CLR}":POKE 53280,0:POKE 53281,
0:PRINT"{WHT}":AR=26:AO=45:AV=8:SP=9
20 PRINT"   WELCOME TO THE ENCHANTED CAT
LE.      "
21 PRINT"   VERSION 1.0    [C] 1984 BY W
ALKOWIAK"
25 PRINT"{CMO}{CMO}{CMO}{CMO}{CMO}{CMO}{
CMO}{CMO}{CMO}{CMO}{CMO}{CMO}{CMO}{CMO}{
CMO}{CMO}{CMO}{CMO}{CMO}{CMO}{CMO}{CMO}{
CMO}{CMO}{CMO}{CMO}{CMO}{CMO}{CMO}{CMO}{
CMO}{CMO}{CMO}{CMO}{CMO}{CMO}{CMO}{CMO}{
CMO}"
30 PRINT:PRINT: PRINT"I AM THY FAITHFUL
SERVANT.":PRINT
35 PRINT"COMMAND ME IN THE FOLLOWING WAY
:":PRINT
40 PRINT"EXAMINE TABLE, PUT BOTTLE":PRIN
T
50 PRINT"ETC. TO TELL ME WHAT TO DO.":PR
INT
60 PRINT"IF YOU WANT TO KNOW WHAT I AM C
ARRYING":PRINT
65 PRINT"USE THE COMMAND INVENTORY."
66 PRINT"{CMO}{CMO}{CMO}{CMO}{CMO}{CMO}{
CMO}{CMO}{CMO}{CMO}{CMO}{CMO}{CMO}{CMO}{
CMO}{CMO}{CMO}{CMO}{CMO}{CMO}{CMO}{CMO}{
CMO}{CMO}{CMO}{CMO}{CMO}{CMO}{CMO}{CMO}{
CMO}{CMO}{CMO}{CMO}{CMO}{CMO}{CMO}{CMO}{
CMO}"
70 PRINT:PRINT
80 PRINT"           ARE YOU READY ?"
85 GETA$:IFA$=""THEN85
90 DIM RA$[AR], DU[AR,6], OB$[AO], RN$[A
O], OB[AO],MS$[11]
101 DATA"IN THE CASTLE LIBRARY.",0,3,0,2
,0,0
102 DATA"IN THE STUDY.",0,0,1,0,0,0
103 DATA"IN THE KITCHEN.",1,8,0,4,0,0
104 DATA"IN THE CASTLE COURTYARD.",0,8,3
,6,0,0
105 DATA"IN ONE OF THE WATCHTOWERS.",0,0
,0,0,0,11
106 DATA"IN THE CASTLE COURTYARD.",11,0,
```

```
4,0,0,0
107 DATA"IN FRONT OF THE DRAWBRIDGE.",0,
0,6,0,0,0
108 DATA"IN THE GREAT HALL.",4,8,3,9,0,0
109 DATA"IN A PRIVATE CHAMBER.",9,9,8,0,
0,0
110 DATA"ON THE DRAWBRIDGE.",0,0,7,12,0,
0
111 DATA"IN THE CASTLE COURTYARD.",0,6,0
,0,5,0
112 DATA"ON A FOREST PATH.",12,16,10,13,
0,0
113 DATA"IN THE ENCHANTED FOREST.",21,17
,12,15,0,0
114 DATA"IN A DARK CAVE.",0,18,14,0,0,0
115 DATA"IN THE FOREST.",15,15,15,16,0,0
116 DATA"IN THE ENCHANTED FOREST.",12,21
,15,17,0,0
117 DATA"IN THE ENCHANTED FOREST.",13,22
,16,18,0,0
118 DATA"AT THE FOOT OF A MOUNTAIN RANGE
.",14,0,17,19,0,0
119 DATA"IN A DARK CAVE.",25,0,18,19,0,0
120 DATA"IN THE CASTLE.",20,20,20,21,0,0
121 DATA"IN THE FOREST.",16,21,20,21,0,0
122 DATA"IN THE BOG.",17,0,0,23,0,0
123 DATA"IN THE BOG.",0,0,22,24,0,0
124 DATA"BY A STREAM.",23,24,0,23,0,0
125 DATA"IN A DARK CAVE.",25,19,25,14,14
,0
126 DATA"IN A SNAKEPIT.",0,0,0,0,22,0
401 DATA"COUNTLESS BOOKSHELVES","SHE",1
402 DATA"A DESK","DES",1
403 DATA"MY TEACHER 'VIC CHIP'.","VIC",2
404 DATA"A COLANDER","COL",3
405 DATA"A BOTTLE","BOT",0
406 DATA"THE CASTLE WELL","WEL",4
407 DATA "BOOK","BOO",0
408 DATA"SLEEPING WATCHMEN","WAT",5
409 DATA"THE DRAWBRIDGE WINDING GEAR","G
EA",5
410 DATA"CASTLE RESIDENTS","RES",8
411 DATA"MY GUESTS",GUE",8
412 DATA"PIECE OF PAPER","PAP",0
413 DATA"A KITCHEN TABLE","TAB",3
414 DATA"A BUTCHERS KNIFE","KNI",0
415 DATA"A CROSSBOW","CRO",5
416 DATA"A KEY","KEY",0
417 DATA"A HEAVY IRON GATE","GAT",6
```

```
418 DATA"A DRAWBRIDGE,",",","DRA",7
419 DATA"NOTHING IN PARTICULAR","NOT",9
420 DATA"NOTHING IN PARTICULAR","NOT",11
421 DATA"TREES","TRE",12
422 DATA"TREES","TRE",13
423 DATA"A LOT OF CABINETS","CAB",14
424 DATA"NOTHING IN PARTICULAR","NOT",25
425 DATA"TREES","TRE",15
426 DATA"TREES","TRE",16
427 DATA"TREES","TRE",17
428 DATA"A LARGE MAGPIE","MAG",17
429 DATA"AN ENTRANCE TO A CAVE","CAV",18
430 DATA"GLEAMING GOLD METAL","GOL", 19
431 DATA"OLD ARMOR","ARM",0
432 DATA"NOTHING IN PARTICULAR","NOT",21
433 DATA"BOG","BOG",0
434 DATA"MUD","MUD",23
435 DATA"SNAKES EGGS","EGG",26
436 DATA"TREACHEROUS GROUND","GRO",23
437 DATA"SPRING OF BUBBLING WATER","SPR"
,24
438 DATA"A MOAT","MOA",10
439 DATA"A DARK CORNER","COR",20
440 DATA"COBWEBS","COB",0
441 DATA"A BOTTLE WITH BLUE WATER IN IT"
,"WAT",0
442 DATA"NOTHING IN PARTICULAR","NOT",19
443 DATA"A SNAKEPIT","PIT",22
444 DATA"SNAKES","SNA",26
445 DATA"A STONE ALTER","ALT",25
800 DATA EXA,TAK,REA,OPE,DES,USE,FIL,PUT
900 MS$[0]="I DON'T UNDERSTAND WHAT YOU
MEAN."
901 MS$[1]="I CAN'T SEE ANYTHING SPECIAL
."
902 MS$[2]="I'M NOT STRONG ENOUGH."
903 MS$[3]="THEY SEEM TO BE FAST ASLEEP.
"
904 MS$[4]="THAT WOULD BE SILLY."
905 MS$[5]="I CAN SEE SOME SHAKY WRITING
."
906 MS$[6]="THE MAGPIE'S STOLEN SOMETHIN
G !"
907 MS$[7]="THERE'S SOME OLD ARMOR."
908 MS$[8]="HE'S GOT A PIECE OF PAPER IN
 HIS HAND."
909 MS$[9]="HE'S GOT A KEY IN HIS HAND."
910 MS$[10]="THERE'S AN INSCRIPTION- IT
SAYS:"
```

```
911 MS$[11]="ACCEPT OUR SACRIFICE AND BE
  GRATEFUL TO US."
950 FOR RA=1 TO AR:READRA$[RA]
952 FOR RI=1 TO 6:READDU[RA,RI]
954 NEXT RI:NEXT RA
961 FOR OB=1 TO AO:READ OB$[OB], RN$[OB]
, OB[OB]:NEXT OB
970 FOR I=1 TO AV:READ VE$[I]:NEXT I
1010 LE$="
          "
1020 DATA NORTH, SOUTH, WEST, EAST, UP,
DOWN
1030 FOR RI=1 TO 6:READ RI$[RI]:NEXT RI
1040 CO=RND[1]
1070 PRINT"{CLR}"
1080 PRINT"{CM4}":POKE211,0:POKE214,0:SY
S58732
1090 POKE211,0:POKE214,0:SYS 58732
1100 FOR Z=1 TO 10:PRINTLE$:NEXT Z
1130 POKE211,0:POKE214,0:SYS 58732
1140 PRINT"I AM ";
1150 PRINTRA$[SP]
1160 PRINT"I CAN SEE ";
1170 FOR I=1 TO AO
1180 IF OB[I]<>SP THEN 1200
1185 IF POS[O]+LEN[OB$[I]]+2<=39 THEN PR
INT OB$[I];", ";:GOTO 1200
1190 IF POS[O]+LEN[OB$[I]]+2>39 THEN PRI
NT
1196 GOTO 1185
1200 NEXT I
1205 PRINT"{LFT}{LFT}."
1210 PRINT
1215 PRINT
1220 PRINT"I CAN GO ";
1230 FOR RI=1 TO 6
1240 IF DU[SP,RI]=0 THEN GOTO 1250
1245 IFPOS[O]=14THENPRINTRI$[RI];:GOTO12
50
1246 IFPOS[O]+LEN[RI$[RI]]<37 THENPRINT"
, ";RI$[RI];:GOTO1250
1247 IFPOS[O]+LEN[RI$[RI]]>37THENPRINT:P
RINTRI$[RI];:GOTO1250
1249 IFPOS[O]<16 AND POS[O]>2 THENPRINT"
, ";RI$[RI];:GOTO1250
1250 NEXT RI
1260 PRINT"."
1270 PRINT"{CMO}{CMO}{CMO}{CMO}{CMO}{CMO
}{CMO}{CMO}{CMO}{CMO}{CMO}{CMO}{CMO}{CMO
```

```
}{CMO}{CMO}{CMO}{CMO}{CMO}{CMO}{CMO}{CMO
}{CMO}{CMO}{CMO}{CMO}{CMO}{CMO}{CMO}{CMO
}{CMO}{CMO}{CMO}{CMO}{CMO}{CMO}{CMO}{CMO
}{CMO}"
1275 IFSP=25THENGOSUB8050
1280 POKE211,0:POKE214,24:SYS 58732:PRIN
T"{WHT}";:INPUT"WHAT SHALL I DO";EI$:PRI
NT"{CM8}";
1285 IFSP=17THENGOSUB9040
1286 IFSP=23THENGOSUB9080
1287 IFSP=15THENGOSUB9100
1290 IFEI$="N"ANDDU(SP,1)<>0THENSP=DU(SP
,1):PRINT"O.K.":GOTO1080
1300 IFEI$="S"ANDDU(SP,2)<>2THENSP=DU(SP
,2):PRINT"O.K.":GOTO1080
1310 IFEI$="W"ANDDU(SP,3)<>0THENSP=DU(SP
,3):PRINT"O.K.":GOTO1080
1320 IFEI$="E"ANDDU(SP,4)<>0THENSP=DU(SP
,4):PRINT"O.K.":GOTO1080
1330 IFEI$="U"ANDDU(SP,5)<>0THENSP=DU(SP
,5):PRINT"O.K.":GOTO1080
1340 IFEI$="D"ANDDU(SP,6)<>0THENSP=DU(SP
,6):PRINT"O.K.":GOTO1080
1350 IF LEN(EI$)<3 THEN PRINT"THAT DOESN
'T LEAD ANYWHERE!":GOTO 1080
1360 IF LEFT$(EI$,3)<>"INV"THENGOTO1990
1370 PRINT"I'M CARRYING THE FOLLOWING:"
1380 FORI=1TOAO:IFOB(I)=-1THENPRINTOB$(I
)
1390 NEXTI
1400 GOTO1080
1990 IFSP=15THENGOSUB9100
2000 LN=LEN(EI$)
2010 FOR EL=1 TO LN:TE$=MID$(EI$,EL,1)
2030 IF TE$<>" "THEN NEXT EL
2040 EV$=LEFT$(EI$,3):RL=LN-EL:IFRL<0THE
N2070
2065 EO$=RIGHT$(EI$,RL)
2066 EO$=LEFT$(EO$,3)
2070 FOR VN=1 TO AV
2080 IF EV$=VE$(VN) THEN 2110
2090 NEXT VN
2100 PRINT"I DON'T UNDERSTAND THE VERB!"
:GOTO 1080
2110 FOR N=1 TO AO
2120 IF EO$=RN$(N) THEN 4000
2130 NEXT N
2140 PRINT"I DON'T UNDERSTAND THE OBJECT
!":GOTO 1080
```

```
4000 ON VN GOTO 5000,5500,5600,5700,5800
,5900,6000,6100
5000 IF OB[N]<>SP AND OB[N]<>-1 THEN GOT
O 5080
5001 IFN=16ANDSP=20ANDOB[31]<>-1ANDOB[40
]<>-1THENPRINTMS$[7]:OB[31]=20:OB[40]=20
:GOTO1080
5002 IF N=10AND SP=8THEN PRINT MS$[3]:GO
TO1080
5003 IF N=11 AND SP=7 THEN PRINT MS$[3]:
GOTO1080
5004 IF N=4  AND[SP=3 OR OB[N]=-1] THEN
PRINT MS$[1]:GOTO1080
5005 IF N=5  AND[SP=3 OR OB[N]=-1] THEN
PRINT MS$[1]:GOTO1080
5006 IF N=1 AND SP=1 THEN PRINT MS$[1]:G
OTO1080
5008 IF N=3 AND SP=2ANDOB[12]=OTHENPRINT
MS$[8]:OB[12]=2:GOTO1080
5009 IFN=3ANDSP=2THENPRINTMS$[1]:GOTO108
O
5010 IFN=6ANDOB[5]=OTHENPRINT"THERE'S A
BOTTLE IN THE WATER.":OB[5]=SP:GOTO1080
5011 IFN=7AND[SP=1OROB[N]=-1]THENPRINT"I
T'S A BOOK ABOUT MAGIC POTIONS.":GOTO108
O
5012 IFN=8ANDSP=5ANDOB[16]=OTHENPRINTMS$
[9]:OB[16]=SP:GOTO1080
5013 IF N=9 AND NOT FL[1] THEN PRINTMS$[
1]:GOTO1080
5014 IF N=9 AND FL[1]ANDSP=5 THENPRINT"I
T WON'T GO/":GOTO1080
5015 IFN=12ANDOB[12]=-1THENPRINT"THERE'S
 SOMETHING WRITTEN ON IT.":OB[16]=SP:GOT
O1080
5016 IFN=12ANDOB[12]=2THENPRINT"I'LL HAV
E TO PICK IT UP FIRST.":GOTO1080
5017 IFN=13ANDOB[14]=OTHENPRINT"THERE'S
A KNIFE ON THE TABLE.":OB[14]=3:GOTO1080
5018 IFN=2AND[OB[7]=1OROB[7]=0]THENPRINT
"THERE'S AN OLD BOOK ON IT.":OB[7]=1:GOT
O1080
5019 IFN=14 AND [OB[14]=SP OR OB[14]=-1]
THENPRINT"THE BLADE'S VERY SHARP":GOTO10
80
5020 IFN=15AND[OB[N]=SPOROB[N]=-1]THENPR
INTMS$[1]:GOTO1080
5021 IFN=16AND[OB[16]=-1OROB[16]=SP]THEN
PRINTMS$[1]:GOTO1080
```

```
5022 IFN=17ANDSP=6ANDFL[3]<>-1THENPRINT"
IT'S CLOSED.":GOTO1080
5023 IFN=17ANDSP=6ANDFL[3]=-1THENPRINT"I
T'S WIDE OPEN.":GOTO1080
5024 IFN=18ANDSP=7ANDFL[1]THENPRINT"DRAW
BRIDGE'S BEING LOWERED.":DU[7,4]=10:GOTO
1080
5025 IFN=18ANDSP=7ANDNOTFL[1]THENPRINT"T
HE DRAWBRIDGE IS UP.":GOTO1080
5026 IFN=21THENPRINTMS$[1]:GOTO1080
5027 IFN=23ANDSP=14GOTO10000
5028 IFN=28ANDSP=17THENPRINT"IT'S REALLY
 A MARVELLOUS COPY.":GOSUB9040:GOTO1080
5029 IFN=29ANDSP=18THENPRINT"THERE'S A F
UNNY SMELL COMING FROM IT.":GOTO1080
5030 IFN=30ANDSP=19OROB[30]=-1THENPRINT"
IT'S USELESS METAL.":GOTO1080
5031 IFN=31AND(SP=20OROB[31]=-1)THENPRIN
TMS$[1]:GOTO1080
5032 IFN=35AND(SP=26OROB[35]=-1)THENPRIN
TMS$[1]:GOTO1080
5033 IFN=36ANDSP=23THENPRINT"IT DOESNT'T
 LOOK LIKE IT WILL BEAR MUCH.":GOTO1080
5034 IFN=37ANDSP=24THENPRINT"IT'S THE FA
MOUS BLUE WATER.":GOTO1080
5035 IFN=38ANDSP=10THENPRINTMS$[1]:GOTO1
080
5036 IFN=40AND(SP=20OROB[40]=-1)THENPRIN
TMS$[1]:GOTO1080
5037 IFN=43THENSP=26:PRINT"O.K.":GOTO108
0
5038 IFN=45 THENPRINTMS$[10]:PRINTMS$[11
]:GOTO1080
5080 IFN=21THENPRINTMS$[1]:GOTO1080
5081 IFN=39ANDSP=20ANDOB[31]<>-1ANDOB[40
]<>-1THENPRINTMS$[7]:OB[31]=20:OB[40]=20
:GOTO1080
5082 IFN=33ANDSP=23THENGOSUB9080:PRINT"T
HERE'S A SPRING IN THE EAST.":GOTO1080
5083 IFN=16AND(SP=23OROB[34]=-1)THENPRIN
T"IT'S MEDICINAL MUD.":GOSUB9080:GOTO108
0
5098 PRINTMS$[1]:GOTO1080
5500 IFOB[N]<>SPANDOB[N]<>-1THENGOTO5580
5501 IFN=1THENPRINTMS[2]:GOTO1080
5502 IFN=6THENPRINTMS[2]:GOTO1080
5503 IFN=17THENPRINTMS$[2]:GOTO1080
5504 IFN=2 THENPRINTMS$[4]:GOTO1080
5505 IFN=3 THENPRINTMS[4]:GOTO1080
```

```
5506 IFN=8 THENPRINTMS$(4):GOTO1080
5507 IFN=10THENPRINTMS$(4):GOTO1080
5508 IFN=11THENPRINTMS$(4):GOTO1080
5509 ZA=0:FORI=1TOAO:IFOB(I)=-1THENZA=ZA
+1:IFZA=4 THENGOTO5599
5510 NEXT I
5511 IFN=5THENOB(N)=-1:PRINT"O.K.":GOTO1
080
5512 IFN=7THENOB(N)=-1:PRINT"O.K.":GOTO1
080
5513 IFN=12THENOB(N)=-1:PRINT"O.K.":GOTO
1080
5514 IFN=15THENOB(N)=-1:PRINT"O.K.":GOTO
1080
5515 IFN=16THENOB(N)=-1:PRINT"O.K.":GOTO
1080
5516 IFN=14THENOB(N)=-1:PRINT"O.K.":GOTO
1080
5517 IFN=9THENPRINTMS$(2):GOTO1080
5518 IFN=23THENPRINTMS$(2):GOTO1080
5519 IFN=28THENPRINT"WHAT SHALL I CATCH
IT WITH?":GOSUB9040:GOTO1080
5520 IFN=18THENPRINTMS$(0):GOTO1080
5521 IFN=30THENOB(N)=-1:PRINT"O.K.":GOTO
1080
5522 IFN=31THENOB(31)=-1:PRINT"I'VE PUT
THE ARMOR ON.":GOTO1080
5523 IFN=35ANDOB(31)=-1THENPRINT"O.K.":O
B(35)=-1:GOTO1080
5524 IFN=35ANDOB(31)<>-1THENGOTO8000
5525 IFN=36THENPRINTMS$(4):GOTO1080
5526 IFN=37ANDOB(5)=-1THENPRINT"O.K.":OB
(5)=0:OB(4)=-1:GOTO1080
5527 IFN=37ANDOB(5)<>-1THENPRINT"I NEED
AN EMPTY BOTTLE FIRST.":GOTO1080
5528 IFN=38THENPRINTMS$(0):GOTO1080
5529 IFN=40THENOB(40)=-1:PRINT"O.K.":GOT
O1080
5532 IFN=13THENPRINTMS$(4):GOTO1080
5533 IFN=4THENOB(N)=-1:PRINT"O.K.":GOTO1
080
5580 IFN=34ANDOB(4)<>-1THENPRINT"I NEED
SOMETHING TO PUT IN.":GOTO1080
5581 IFN=34ANDOB(4)=-1THENPRINT"O.K.":OB
(34)=-1:GOTO1080
5589 PRINT"I CAN'T SEE ANYTHING LIKE THA
T HERE.":GOTO1080
5590 GOTO1080
5599 PRINT"SORRY, BUT I CAN'T CARRY ANYM
```

```
ORE !":GOTO1080
5600 IFN=12ANDOB[12]<>-1THENPRINT"I HAVE
N'T GOT A PIECE OF PAPER.":GOTO1080
5601 IFN=12ANDOB[12]=-1THENCO$=RIGHT$[ST
R$[TI],3]:CO=VAL[CO$]:PRINTMS$[5];CO :GO
TO1080
5602 IFN=7ANDOB[7]=-1THENGOTO5650
5603 IFN=7ANDOB[7]<>-1THENPRINT"I'VE GOT
 TO HAVE IT FIRST.":GOTO1080
5649 GOTO1080
5650 INPUT"WHICH PAGE";SE
5651 IF SE<>COTHENPRINTMS$[1]:GOTO1080
5652 PRINT"{CLR}":PRINTSPC[2]"ADVICE FOR
 CERTAIN EMERGENCIES.":PRINT
5654 PRINT"IF YOU FIND THAT A WICKED WIT
CH HAS PUT";
5655 PRINT"ALL YOUR FAMILY AND FRIENDS I
NTO A LONG SLEEP THEN LET ME GIVE YOU ";
5656 PRINT"SOME ADVICE:"
5657 PRINT:PRINT:PRINT"GET HOLD OF
 THE INGREDIENTS FOR THE"
5658 PRINT"WIZARD'S FAVORITE TREAT AND T
HEN BRING"
5659 PRINT"THEM TO HIM ON THE FAR SIDE O
F THE WOOD.";
5660 PRINT"IF HE FEELS LIKE IT, HE WILL
HELP YOU,"
5661 PRINT"FAILING THAT YOU WILL HAVE TO
 WAIT FOR"
5662 PRINT"A PRINCE TO COME AND BRING AL
L THE "
5663 PRINT"PEOPLE IN THE CASTLE BACK TO
LIFE WITH A KISS."
5665 GETA$:IFA$=""THEN5665
5666 PRINT"{CLR}"
5667 PRINT"{ DN}THE INGREDIENTS ARE AS F
OLLOWS"
5668 PRINT"{SH*}{SH*}{SH*}{SH*}{SH*}{SH*
}{SH*}{SH*}{SH*}{SH*}{SH*}{SH*}{SH*}{SH*
}{SH*}{SH*}{SH*}{SH*}{SH*}{SH*}{SH*}{SH*
}{SH*}{SH*}{SH*}{SH*}{SH*}{SH*}{SH*}{SH*
}{SH*}"
5669 PRINT"{ DN}SPIDER WEBS"
5670 PRINT"{ DN}SNAKE EGGS"
5671 PRINT"{ DN}MEDICINAL MUD"
5672 PRINT"{ DN}BLENDED WITH THE MAGIC W
ATER"
5673 PRINT"{ DN}{ DN}JUST PRESENT THESE
TO THE WIZARD."
```

```
5674 GETA$:IFA$=""THEN5674
5675 PRINT"{CLR}":GOTO1080
5700 IFN=17ANDOB[16]<>-1THENPRINT"WHAT W
ITH ?":GOTO1080
5701 IFN=17ANDOB[16]=-1THENPRINT"O.K.":D
U[6,4]=7:FL[3]=-1:GOTO1080
5702 IFN=35ANDOB[35]THENPRINT"THERE'S A
THICK LIQUID IN IT.":GOTO1080
5799 GOTO1080
5800 IFN=9ANDOB[14]=-1ANDSP=5THENPRINT"T
HE HOLDING ROPES HAVE BEEN CUT.":FL[1]=-
1:GOTO1080
5801 IFN=9ANDSP=5ANDOB[14]<>-1THENPRINT"
WHAT WITH ??":GOTO1080
5899 PRINTMS$[0]:GOTO1080
5900 IFOB[N]<>SPANDOB[N]<>-1THENPRINT"I
CAN'T SEE ANYTHING LIKE THAT !":GOTO1080
5901 IFN=9THENPRINT"YOU NEED AT LEAST TW
O MEN FOR THAT JOB.":GOTO1080
5902 IFOB[14]=-1ANDSP=5THENPRINT"THE HOL
DING ROPES HAVE BEEN CUT.":FL[1]=-1 :GOT
O1080
5903 IFN=31THENPRINT"O.K. - I HAVE GOT T
HE ARMOR ON.":OB[N]=-1:GOTO1080
6000 IFN=5ANDSP=24ANDOB[5]=-1THENPRINT"O
.K.":OB[5]=0:OB[41]=-1:GOTO1080
6010 IFN=5ANDOB[5]=-1ANDSP<>24THENPRINT"
WHAT WITH ?":GOTO1080
6020 PRINT"I CAN'T":GOTO1080
6100 IFOB[N]<>-1THENGOTO6180
6101 IFN=4THENPRINT"O.K.":OB[N]=SP:GOTO1
080
6102 IFN=5THENPRINT"O.K.":OB[N]=SP:GOTO1
080
6103 IFN=7THENPRINT"O.K.":OB[N]=SP:GOTO1
080
6104 IFN=12THENPRINT"O.K.":OB[N]=SP:GOTO
1080
6105 IFN=15THENPRINT"O.K.":OB[N]=SP:GOTO
1080
6106 IFN=16THENPRINT"O.K.":OB[N]=SP:GOTO
1080
6107 IFN=14THENPRINT"O.K.":OB[N]=SP:GOTO
1080
6108 IFN=30THENPRINT"O.K.":OB[N]=SP:GOTO
1080
6109 IFN=41THENPRINT"O.K.":OB[N]=SP:GOTO
1080
6110 IFN=45THENPRINT"O.K.":OB[N]=SP:GOTO
```

```
1080
6111 IFN=40THENPRINT"O.K.":OB[N]=SP:GOTO
1080
6112 IFN=36THENPRINT"O.K.":OB[N]=SP:GOTO
1080
6113 IFN=35THENPRINT"O.K.":OB[N]=SP:GOTO
1080
6114 IFN=31THENPRINT"O.K.":OB[N]=SP:GOTO
1080
6170 GOTO1080
6180 IFN=5ANDOB[41]=-1THENPRINT"O.K.":OB
[41]=SP:GOTO1080
6181 IFN=4ANDOB[34]=-1THENPRINT"O.K.":OB
[34]=SP:OB[4]=SP:GOTO1080
6190 GOTO1080
8000 PRINT"{CLR}":PRINT"A SNAKE'S BITTEN
 ME."
8010 PRINT"I HAVE BEEN KILLED.":PRINT:PR
INT"SHALL I TRY AGAIN ?"
8020 GETA$:IFA$=""THEN8020
8030 IF A$="N"THENEND
8040 RUN
8050 IFOB[34]<>25THENRETURN
8060 IFOB[35]<>25THENRETURN
8070 IFOB[41]<>25THENRETURN
8080 IFOB[40]<>25THENRETURN
8090 PRINT"{CLR}":PRINT"{CM4}I CAN HEAR
A VOICE":PRINT:PRINT:PRINT
8100 PRINT"{CM4}THE OLD HUMBUG'S DELIGHT
ED WITH YOUR"
8110 PRINT:PRINT"PRESENTS. HE IS GOING T
O USE HIS MAGIC"
8120 PRINT:PRINT"TO HELP YOU.":PRINT:PRI
NT
8130 PRINT"GO BACK HOME WHERE A FEAST IS
 PREPARED":PRINT
8140 PRINT"TO CELEBRATE THE END OF LONG
SLEEP !";:PRINT
8160 GOTO8160
8170 PRINT"{CLR}"
9040 IFOB[30]=-1THENOB[30]=20:PRINTMS$[6
]:RETURN
9050 IFOB[35]=-1THENOB[35]=20:PRINTMS$[6
]:RETURN
9060 IFOB[5]=-1THENOB[5]=20:PRINTMS$[6]:
RETURN
9070 RETURN
9080 IFOB[31]<>-1THENRETURN
9090 PRINT"{CLR}":PRINT"I'M TOO HEAVY AN
```

```
D I'M SINKING !":GOTO8010
9100 IFRND(1)>.3THENRETURN
9110 PRINT"{CLR}": PRINT"I'VE FALLEN IN
TO A TRAP.":GOTO8010
10000 PRINT"{CLR}":PRINT"IT'S AN ENCHANT
ED KITCHEN, THE WIZARDS"
10010 PRINT"COMING AND HE'S GOING TO TUR
N ME INTO STONE.":GOTO8010

READY.
```

```
0 REM   C64 ADVENTURE EDITOR
1 REM[C]  1984  BY J. WALKOWIAK
2 REM-----------------------------------
-----------
5 POKE 53280,0: POKE 53281,0: PRINT"{YEL
}"
7 A$(0)="ADVENTURE SYSTEM 1.0"
8 A$(1)="[C]1984 BY WALKOWIAK":A$(2)="FR
OM THE ABACUS BOOK"
9 A$(3)="ADVENTURE GAMEWRITER'S HANDBOOK
"
10 PRINT"{CLR}{ DN}{ DN}":FORI=0TO4:PRIN
TSPC(20-INT(LEN(A$(I))/2))A$(I)"{ DN}":N
EXT
11 DIM RA$(60),OB$(60),OB(60),VE$(30),MS
$(60),AC$(30,60),BC$(30,60),RN$(60)
15 DIM AD$(20),DU(60,6)
16 M1$="ADVENTURE EDITOR    VER 1.0"
17 M2$="{ DN}{ DN}{WHT}WHAT WOULD YOU LI
KE?"
18 M3$="{SH*}{SH*}{SH*}{SH*}{SH*}{SH*}{S
H*}{SH*}{SH*}{SH*}{SH*}{SH*}{SH*}{SH*}{S
H*}{SH*}{SH*}{SH*}{SH*}{SH*}{SH*}{SH*}{S
H*}{SH*}{SH*}{SH*}{SH*}{SH*}{SH*}{SH*}{S
H*}{SH*}{SH*}{SH*}{SH*}{SH*}{SH*}{SH*}{S
H*}{SHC}"
19 M4$="
"
20 AR=0:AO=0:AV=0:AM=0:AF=0:I2=1:L3=1
25 FORI=1TO2000:NEXTI
30 PRINT"{CLR}";M1$:PRINTM3$
40 PRINT"{ DN}{ DN}WHICH ADVENTURE DO YO
U WISH TO PROCESS":INPUT NA$:INPUT"{ DN}
VERSION ";VE$
50 INPUT"{ DN}COPYRIGHT BY ";CR$
200 PRINT"{CLR}{YEL}";M1$:PRINT M3$;
210 PRINTSPC(10)"{CM8}0 - IDENTIFICATION
 DATA"
211 PRINTTAB(10)"{ DN}1 - ENTER ROOMS
"
212 PRINTTAB(10)"{ DN}2 - ENTER OBJECTS
"
213 PRINTTAB(10)"{ DN}3 - ENTER VERBS
```

```
"
214 PRINTTAB[10]"[ DN]4 - OBJECT POSITIO
NS"
215 PRINTTAB[10]"[ DN]5 - CONNECT ROOMS
TOGETHER"
216 PRINTTAB[10]"[ DN]6 - CONDITIONS & A
CTIONS "
217 PRINTTAB[10]"[ DN]7 - INSERT MESSAGE
S"
218 PRINTTAB[10]"[ DN]8 - DISK ACCESS
"
219 PRINTTAB[10]"[ DN]9 - PROGRAM END   "
220 PRINTM3$
225 PRINTTAB[10]"PLEASE CHOOSE      "
230 GOSUB10000
235 IF A=9 THEN EN=-1:GOTO 5100
240 ON A+1 GOTO 3000,1100,1200,1300,1400
,1500,1600,4000,5000,6000
499 REM ------ I/O ROUTINE
500 PRINT"[CLR]";
510 ZE=0:SP=0:GOSUB 11000:PRINT T1$
520 Z=Z+1
555 ZE=0:SP=25:GOSUB 11000:PRINTT2$;Z
556 PRINTM3$
557 ZE=16:SP=0:GOSUB 11000:PRINT M4$
558 ZE=16:SP=0:GOSUB 11000:PRINTZ-1;:IF
A=1 THEN PRINT RA$[Z-1]
559 IF A=2 THEN PRINT OB$[Z-1]
560 IF A=3 THEN PRINT VERB$[Z-1]
563 ZE=20:SP=0:GOSUB 11000:PRINTT3$;:EI$
="":INPUT EI$:IFEI$=""THEN563
564 IF LEFT$[EI$,1]="*"THEN GOTO 200
565 IF A=2 THEN ZE=22:SP=0:GOSUB 11000:I
NPUT"OBJECT NAME ";RN$[Z]
570 ZE=20:SP=0:GOSUB 11000:PRINT M4$
571 ZE=22:SP=0:GOSUB 11000:PRINT M4$
590 RETURN
1100 PRINT"[CLR]":T1$="ENTER ROOMS ":T2$
=" ROOM NO.;":T3$="I AM "
1105 Z=AR
1110 GOSUB 510 :REM PRINT ROOMS
1120 RA$[Z]=EI$
1125 AR=Z
1130 GOTO 1110
1199 REM --------------- END
```

```
1200 PRINT"{CLR}":T1$="ENTER OBJECTS ":T
2$=" OBJECT NO":T3$="I SEE "
1205 Z=AO
1210 GOSUB 510
1220 OB$(Z)=EI$
1225 AO=Z
1230 GOTO1210
1290 REM --------------- END INPUT OBJEC
TS
1300 PRINT"{CLR}"
1301 T1$="ENTER VERBS":T2$="VERB NO.:"
1302 T3$=""
1305 Z=AV
1310 GOSUB 510
1320 VERB$(Z)=EI$
1330 AV=Z
1360 GOTO 1310
1390 REM ----------
1399 REM -------------------- OBJECT LO
CATIONS
1400 PRINT"{CLR}"
1410 LP=L3
1420 FOR I=LP TO AO
1430 GOSUB 12000      :REM PRINT LIST
1440 ZE=23:SP=0:GOSUB11000:PRINT"OBJECT
  ";RN$(I);"   IN ROOM NO.";:INPUT OB(I)
1450 LP=I+1
1460 PRINT"{CLR}"
1470 NEXT I
1490 GOTO 200
1500 FOR R1=I2 TO AR
1510 PRINT"{CLR}"
1520 GOSUB 12000
1530 PRINT"( DN)ROOM";R1;"LEADS NORTH TO
";:INPUT DU(R1,1)
1540 PRINT"( DN)ROOM";R1;"LEADS SOUTH TO
";:INPUT DU(R1,2)
1550 PRINT"( DN)ROOM";R1;"LEADS WEST TO"
;:INPUT DU(R1,3)
1560 PRINT"( DN)ROOM";R1;"LEADS EAST TO"
;:INPUT DU(R1,4)
1570 PRINT"( DN)ROOM";R1;"LEADS UP TO";:
INPUT DU(R1,5)
1580 PRINT"( DN)ROOM";R1;"LEADS DOWN TO"
;:INPUT DU(R1,6)
```

```
1585 NEXT R1
1590 GOTO200
1591 REM -------------------- END CONNECT
IONS
1600 PRINT"{CLR}": REM ------------- CON
DITONS AND ACTIONS
1605 NB=0
1607 NB=NB+1
1608 IF NB>AV THEN GOTO 200
1609 RNS[0]="<CONTINUE>"
1610 PRINT"{CLR}":FORI=0 TO A0
1620 PRINT I;RN$[I];
1630 IF POS[0]+LEN[RN$[I+1]]=> 38 THEN P
RINT
1640 NEXT I
1650 PRINT: PRINT M3$:PRINT"{ DN}"
1700 PRINT"ACTION ON VERB   ";VERB$[NB];
"  AND OBJECT NO. ";
1710 INPUT OB
1715 IF OB=0 THEN GOTO 1607
1800 PRINT"{CLR}";
1810 PRINT"PLEASE INSERT ALL CONDITIONS
FOR ACTION   ";VE$[NB];" ";RN$[OB]; "
1815 PRINTM3$
1820 PRINT"{ DN}{ DN}"TAB[5]"R   - OBJEC
T IS IN ROOM"
1830 PRINTTAB[5]"{ DN}I   - OBJECT IS IN
 INVENTORY"
1840 PRINTTAB[5]"{ DN}N   - OBJECT IS NO
T HERE"
1850 PRINTTAB[5]"{ DN}FX  - FLAG X IS SE
T"
1860 PRINTTAB[5]"{ DN}GX  - FLAG X IS DE
LETED"
1870 PRINTTAB[5]"{ DN}SXX - PLAYER IS RO
OM XX "
1880 ZE=20:SP=0:GOSUB11000
1890 PRINT M3$;:PRINT"ALTER CODE ---> ";
BC$[NB,OB]:PRINT
1900 INPUT"CONDITIONS";BC$[NB,OB]
1905 PRINT"{CLR}";VE$[NB];" ";OB$[OB];"
BRINGS ABOUT WHEN:"
1906 PRINTBC$[NB,OB];"  COMPLETES THE FO
LLOWING ACTION:":PRINTM3$;
1910 PRINT"     V  - ";RN$[OB];" DISAPP
```

```
EARS"
1920 PRINTTAB[5]"[ DN]I    - ";RN$[OB];"
GOES INTO INVENTORY"
1930 PRINTTAB[5]"[ DN]NXX - OBJECT XX AP
PEARS NEW"
1940 PRINTTAB[5]"[ DN]DXY - PASSAGE N. T
O ROOM XX"
1950 PRINT TAB[5]"[ DN]DXXY - PASSAGE TO
ROOM XX DIR. Y"
1960 PRINTTAB[5]"[ DN]FX  - SET FLAG X"
1970 PRINTTAB[5]"[ DN]LX  - DELETE FLAG
X"
1980 PRINTTAB[5]"[ DN]MXX - OUTPUT MESSA
GE XX"
1990 PRINTTAB[5]"[ DN]T    - PLAYER DIES"
2000 PRINTTAB[5]"[ DN]E   E END, BECAUSE
 WON"
2005 PRINTM3$;
2010 PRINT"ALTER CODE ---> ";AC$[NB,OB]
2020 INPUT"ACTION";AC$[NB,OB]
2030 GOTO1610
2040 REM ------- END ACTION & CONDITIONS
2080 GOSUB10000
2999 REM -------------------- KENNDATE
N
3000 PRINT"[CLR]IDENTIFICATION FOR THE A
DVENTURE    ";NA$
3010 PRINT"[ DN]"M3$"[ DN]"
3020 PRINT"[ DN]ROOMS:       ";AR
3030 PRINT"[ DN]OBJECTS:     ";AO
3040 PRINT"[ DN]VERBS:       ";AV
3050 PRINT"[ DN]CONDITIONS:";NB
3060 PRINT"[ DN]MESSAGES    ";AM;"[ DN]"
3070 IF LO THEN PRINT"[ DN]";AF;"USED FL
AGS"
3080 PRINTM3$
3090 PRINT"[ DN]START ROOM FOR PLAYER:
 ";SP
3095 PRINT"[ DN]NECESSARY INPUT LENGTH:
 ";WL
3100 GOSUB10000
3110 GOTO200
3999 REM -------------------- INFORM
ATION
4000 PRINT"[CLR]INPUT MESSAGES"
```

```
4010 PRINTM3$
4020 AM=AM+1
4030 PRINT AM;:INPUT MS$[AM]:IF MS$[AM]=
""THEN PRINT"{ UP}{ UP}":GOTO4030
4040 IF LEFT$[MS$[AM],1]="*"THEN AM=AM-1
 : GOTO 200
4050 GOTO 4020
4060 REM -------------------- END OF IN
FO
4999 REM ---------------------- DISK CO
MMANDS
5000 PRINT"{CLR}1 - SAVE"
5010 PRINT"{ DN}2 - LOAD"
5020 GOSUB 10000
5030 IF A<1 OR A>2 THEN GOTO 5020
5040 ON A GOTO 5100, 5500
5100 PRINT"{CLR}PLEASE WAIT ...";:PRINT"
{ DN}SAVING DATA !"
5105 GOSUB6000
5110 OPEN 2,8,2, "@0:"+NA$+",S,W"
5120 PRINT#2,NA$:PRINT#2,VERS$:PRINT#2,C
R$:PRINT#2,WL
5130 PRINT#2,AR:PRINT#2,AO:PRINT#2,AV:PR
INT#2,AM:PRINT#2,SP:PRINT#2,AF
5140 FOR I=1 TO AR:PRINT#2,RA$[I]:NEXT I
5150 FOR I=1 TO AO:PRINT#2,OB$[I]:PRINT#
2,RN$[I]:PRINT#2,OB[I]:NEXT I
5170 FOR I=1 TO AV:PRINT#2,VE$[I]:NEXT I
5180 FOR I=1 TO AM:PRINT#2,MS$[I]:NEXT I
5190 FOR X=1 TO AR
5200 FOR Y=1 TO 6
5210 PRINT#2,DU[X,Y]
5220 NEXT Y
5230 NEXT X
5240 FOR X=1 TO AV
5250 FOR Y=1 TO AO
5255 IFBC$[X,Y]=""THENBC$[X,Y]="*"
5260 PRINT#2,BC$[X,Y]
5270 NEXT Y
5280 NEXT X
5290 FOR X=1 TO AV
5300 FOR Y=1 TO AO
5305 IFAC$[X,Y]=""THENAC$[X,Y]="*"
5310 PRINT#2,AC$[X,Y]
5320 NEXT Y
5330 NEXT X
5340 CLOSE 2 : IF EN THEN PRINT"{CLR}":E
ND
```

```
ND
5350 GOTO 200
5500 PRINT"{CLR}PLEASE WAIT ..":LO=-1 :P
RINT"{ DN}LOADING DATA !"
5510 OPEN 2,8,2,NA$+",S,R"
5520 INPUT#2,NA$:INPUT#2,VERS$:INPUT#2,C
R$:INPUT#2,WL
5530 INPUT#2,AR:INPUT#2,AO:INPUT#2,AV:IN
PUT#2,AM:INPUT#2,SP:INPUT#2,AF
5540 FOR I=1 TO AR:INPUT#2,RA$(I):NEXT I
5550 FOR I=1 TO AO:INPUT#2,OB$(I):INPUT#
2,RN$(I):INPUT#2,OB(I):NEXT I
5570 FOR I=1 TO AV:INPUT#2,VE$(I):NEXT I
5580 FOR I=1 TO AM:INPUT#2,MS$(I):NEXT I
5590 FOR X=1 TO AR
5600 FOR Y=1 TO 6
5610 INPUT#2,DU(X,Y)
5620 NEXT Y
5630 NEXT X
5640 FOR X=1 TO AV
5650 FOR Y=1 TO AO
5660 INPUT#2,BC$(X,Y)
5670 NEXT Y
5680 NEXT X
5690 FOR X=1 TO AV
5700 FOR Y=1 TO AO
5710 INPUT#2,AC$(X,Y)
5720 NEXT Y
5730 NEXT X
5740 CLOSE 2
5750 GOTO 200
5999 REM -------------------------- MOR
E DATA
6000 PRINT"{CLR}PLEASE INSERT THE REST O
F THE DATA:":PRINTM3$
6010 INPUT"{ DN}{ DN}WORD LENGTH";WL
6020 INPUT"{ DN}{ DN}START ROOM ";SP
6030 INPUT"{ DN}{ DN}NUMBER OF FLAGS";AF
6090 RETURN
10000 GET A$:IFA$="" THEN 10000
10010 A=VAL(A$):RETURN
11000 POKE 211,SP:POKE 214,ZE:SYS 58732:
RETURN
12000 SP=0:ZE=0:GOSUB11000
12010 PRINT"LIST OF POSSIBLE ROOMS:":PRI
```

```
NTM3$
12020 FOR I1=1 TO AR:REM          PRINT ROO
M LIST
12030 PRINTI1;RA$[I1];
12040 IF POS[0]+LEN[RA$[I1+1]]->38 THEN
PRINT
12050 NEXT I1
12060 PRINT"( DN)"
12070 RETURN

READY.
```

```
0 REM -- ADVENTURE INTERPRETER VER 1.0
1 REM [C] 1984  BY JOERG WALKOWIAK
2 REM----------------------------------
5 POKE 53281,0:POKE 53281,0
6 PRINT"{CLR}"SPC[10]"ADVENTURE SYSTEM
 1.0"
7 PRINT"           [C] 1984 BY WALKOWIAK"
8 PRINT"{ DN}           FROM THE ABACUS B
OOK"
9 PRINT"{ DN}    ADVENTURE GAMEWRITER'S H
ANDBOOK"
30 FOR I-1TO2000:NEXTI
40 PRINT" WHICH ADVENTURE DO YOU WANT TO
 PLAY":INPUT"  FILE NAME: ";NA$
50 OPEN 2,8,2,NA$+",S,R"
60 INPUT#2,NA$:PRINTNA$:INPUT#2,VERS$:PR
INTVERS$:INPUT#2,CR$:PRINTCR$:INPUT#2,WL
70 INPUT#2,AR:INPUT#2,AO:INPUT#2,AV:INPU
T#2,AM:INPUT#2,SP:INPUT#2,AF
75 DIM RA$[AR],OB$[AO],RN$[AO],OB[AO],VE
$[AV],MS$[AM],AC$[AV,AO],BC$[AV,AO]
76 DIM AD$[20],DU[AR,6]
80 FOR I-1 TO AR:INPUT#2,RA$[I]:NEXTI
90 FORI-1TOAO:INPUT#2,OB$[I]:INPUT#2,RN$
[I]:RN$[I]-LEFT$[RN$[I],WL]:INPUT#2,OB[I
]:NEXTI
100 FOR I-1 TO AV:INPUT#2,VE$[I]:VE$[I]-
LEFT$[VE$[I],WL]: NEXT I
110 FOR I-1 TO AM:INPUT#2,MS$[I]:NEXTI
120 FOR X-1 TO AR : FOR Y-1 TO 6
130 INPUT#2,DU[X,Y]
140 NEXT Y:NEXT X
150 FOR X-1 TO AV : FOR Y-1 TO AO
160 INPUT#2,BC$[X,Y]
170 NEXT Y : NEXT X
180 FOR X-1 TO AV : FOR Y-1 TO AO
190 INPUT#2,AC$[X,Y]
200 NEXT Y : NEXT X
210 CLOSE2
1000 PRINT"{CLR}":PRINT CHR$[142]
1010 LE$-"
       "
```

```
1020 DATA NORTH,SOUTH,WEST,EAST,UP,DOWN
1030 FOR RI=1 TO 6
1040 READ RI$[RI]
1050 NEXT RI
1070 PRINT"{CLR}":POKE 53281,0:POKE53281
,0
1080 PRINT" "
1090 POKE 211,0:POKE 214,0: SYS 58732
1100 FOR ZE=1 TO 10
1110 PRINT LE$
1120 NEXT ZE
1130 POKE 211,0:POKE 214,0: SYS 58732
1140 PRINT"I AM ";
1150 PRINTRA$[SP]
1160 PRINT"I SEE ";:GE=0
1170 FOR I=1 TO AO
1180 IF OB[I]<>SP THEN 1210
1190 IF POS[0]+LEN[OB$[I]]+2 < 39 THEN P
RINT OB$[I];", ";:GE=-1:GOTO 1210
1200 IF POS[0]+LEN[OB$[I]]+2 >= 39 THEN
PRINT : GOTO 1190
1210 NEXT I : IF NOT GE THEN PRINT"NOTHI
NG IN PARTICULAR   ";
1220 PRINT"{LFT}{LFT}."
1230 PRINT LE$
1240 PRINT" I CAN GO ";
1250 FOR RI=1 TO 6
1260 IF DU[SP,RI]=0 THEN GOTO 1310
1270 IF POS[0]=14 THEN PRINT RI$[RI];:GO
TO 1310
1280 IF POS[0]+LEN[RI$[RI]]<37 THEN PRIN
T", ";RI$[RI];:GOTO 1310
1290 IF POS[0]+LEN[RI$[RI]]>=37 THEN PRI
NT", ":PRINTRI$[RI];:GOTO 1310
1300 IF POS[0]<16 AND POS[0]>2 THEN PRIN
T", ";RI$[RI];
1310 NEXT RI
1320 PRINT"."
1330 PRINT" ---------------------------
------"
1390 POKE 211,0:POKE 214,24:SYS 58732:PR
INT" ";:INPUT"WHAT SHALL I DO ";EI$: PRI
NT" ";
1425 IF LEN[EI$]>2 THEN 1500
1430 IF EI$="N"ANDDU[SP,1]<>0 THEN SP=DU
```

```
(SP,1):PRINT"O.K.":GOTO 1080
1440 IF EI$="S"ANDDU(SP,2)<>O THEN SP=DU
(SP,2):PRINT"O.K.":GOTO 1080
1450 IF EI$="W"ANDDU(SP,3)<>O THEN SP=DU
(SP,3):PRINT"O.K.":GOTO 1080
1460 IF EI$="E"ANDDU(SP,4)<>O THEN SP=DU
(SP,4):PRINT"O.K.":GOTO 1080
1470 IF EI$="U"ANDDU(SP,5)<>O THEN SP=DU
(SP,5):PRINT"O.K.":GOTO 1080
1480 IF EI$="D"ANDDU(SP,6)<>O THEN SP=DU
(SP,6):PRINT"O.K.":GOTO 1080
1490 PRINT"THAT DOESN'T LEAD ANYWHERE!":
GOTO1080
1500 IF LEFT$(EI$,3)<>"INV"THEN 1600
1510 PRINT"I AM CARRYING THE FOLLOWING:"
1520 FOR I=1 TO AO
1530 IF OB(I)=-1 THEN PRINT OB$(I)
1540 NEXT I
1550 GOTO 1080
1600 IF LEFT$(EI$,4)<>"SAVE"THEN 1700
1605 PRINT"(CLR)"SPC(10)" SAVE GAME "
1606 INPUT"( DN)( DN)ENTER NAME   ";EI$
1610 IF LEN(EI$)>16 THEN 1605
1615 PRINT"( DN)( DN)FILE ";EI$;" IS SAV
ING."
1620 OPEN 2,8,2,"@0:"+EI$+",S,W"
1625 PRINT#2,NA$:PRINT#2,SP:PRINT#2,FL
1630 FOR I=1 TO AO:PRINT#2,OB(I):NEXTI
1640 FOR RA=1 TO AR:FOR RI=1 TO 6
1650 PRINT#2,DU(RA,RI)
1660 NEXT RI: NEXT RA
1670 FOR I=1 TO AF: PRINT#2,FL(I):NEXT I
1675 CLOSE2:GOSUB 1680:PRINT"(CLR)":GOTO
1080
1680 OPEN1,8,15:INPUT#1,A,B$,C,D
1685 IFA<>OTHENPRINT:PRINTB$:FORI=1TO500
0:NEXT:CLOSE2:CLOSE1:GOTO1080
1690 CLOSE1:RETURN
1700 IF LEFT$(EI$,4)<> "LOAD"THEN 2000
1705 PRINT"(CLR)"SPC(10)" LOAD GAME "
1706 INPUT"( DN)( DN)ENTER NAME";EI$
1710 IF LEN(EI$)>16 THEN 1705
1715 PRINT"( DN)( DN)FILE ";EI$;" IS LOA
DING"
1720 OPEN 2,8,2,"@0:"+EI$+",S,R"
```

```
1725 INPUT#2,NA$:INPUT#2,SP:INPUT#2,FL
1730 FOR I=1 TO AO:INPUT#2,OB[I]:NEXTI
1740 FOR RA=1 TO AR:FOR RI=1 TO 6
1750 INPUT#2,DU[RA,RI]
1760 NEXT RI: NEXT RA
1770 FOR I=1 TO AF: INPUT#2,FL[I]:NEXT I
1775 CLOSE2:GOSUB 1680:PRINT"{CLR}":GOTO
1080
2000 LN=LEN[EI$]
2010 FOR EL=1 TO LN
2020 TE$=MID$[EI$,EL,1]
2030 IF TE$<>" "THEN NEXT EL
2040 EV$=LEFT$[EI$,WL]
2050 RL=LN-EL
2060 IF RL<0 THEN 2090
2070 EO$=RIGHT$[EI$,RL]:EO$=LEFT$[EO$,WL
]
2090 FOR VN=1 TO AV
2100 IF EV$=VE$[VN] THEN 2130
2110 NEXT VN
2120 PRINT"I DON'T UNDERSTAND THE VERB."
:GOTO1080
2130 FOR N=1 TO AO
2140 IF EO$=RN$[N] THEN 2200
2150 NEXT N
2160 PRINT"I DON'T UNDERSTAND THE OBJECT
.":GOTO1080
2198 REM -------------------------------
------ VN AND N AREA VERB/OBJECT NUMBER
2199 REM ------------- CONDITIONS FULFIL
LED
2200 FOR AB=1 TO LEN [BC$[VN,N]]
2210 BD$[AB]=MID$[BC$[VN,N],AB,1]
2220 NEXT AB
2250 FOR AA=1 TO LEN[AC$[VN,N]]
2260 AD$[AA]=MID$[AC$[VN,N],AA,1]
2270 NEXT AA
2280 REM --- CONDITIONS IN BD$     ACTION
S IN AD$ ----
2290 AB=AB-1:AA=AA-1
2300 X=0:ER=0
2310 X=X+1
2320 IF X=AB+1 THEN 2500: REM -----------
------- ALL CONDITIONS CHECKED ----
2330 IF BD$[X]<>"R"THEN 2350
```

```
2340 IF OB[N]<>SP THEN ER=-1 : GOTO 2310
2345 GOTO2310
2350 IF BD$[X]<>"I"THEN 2370
2360 IF OB[N]<>-1 THEN ER=-1 : GOTO 2310
2370 IF BD$[X]<>"N"THEN 2390
2380 IF [OB[N]<>SP AND OB[N]<>-1] THEN E
R=-1 : GOTO 2310
2390 IF BD$[X]<>"S"THEN 2410
2400 R1$=BD$[X+1]+BD$[X+2]:X=X+2:IF SP<>
VAL[R1$] THEN ER=-1 : GOTO 2310
2410 IF BD$[X]<>"F" THEN 2450
2420 IF FL[VAL[BD$[X+1]]]=-1THEN 2440
2430 X=X+1:GOTO 2450
2440 ER=-1:X=X+1:GOTO 2310
2450 IF BD$[X]<>"G" THEN 2310
2460 IF NOT FL[VAL[BD$[X+1]]] THEN 2480
2470 X=X+1:GOTO 2310
2480 ER=-1:X=X+1:GOTO 2310
2490 GOTO 2310
2500 IF NOT ER THEN PRINT"YOU CAN'T DO T
HAT YET.":GOTO 1080
3999 REM ---- ALL CONDIT. FULFILLED
4000 PRINT"O.K."
4999 REM ----------- EXECUTE ACTION
5000 X=0:ER=0
5040 X=X+1
5050 IF X>AA THEN 1080
5060 IF AD$[X]<>"V" THEN 5080
5070 OB[N]=0:GOTO 5040
5080 IF AD$[X]<>"I" THEN 5100
5090 OB[N]=-1:GOTO 5040
5100 IF AD$[X]<>"N" THEN 5120
5110 GOSUB 5500:OB[PA]=SP:GOTO 5040
5120 IF AD$[X]<>"F" THEN 5140
5130 GOSUB 5600:FL[PA]=-1:GOTO 5040
5140 IF AD$[X]<>"L" THEN 5160
5150 GOSUB 5600:FL[PA]=0 :GOTO 5040
5160 IF AD$[X]<>"M" THEN 5180
5170 GOSUB 5500:PRINTMS$[PA] :GOTO 5040
5180 IF AD$[X]<>"E" THEN 5200
5190 GOTO 6000
5200 IF AD$[X]<>"D"THEN 5300
5210 GOTO 5310
5220 DU[SP,P1]=P2
5230 IF P1=1 THEN P3=2
5240 IF P1=2 THEN P3=1
```

```
5250 IF P1=3 THEN P3=4
5260 IF P1=4 THEN P3=3
5270 IF P1=5 THEN P3=6
5280 IF P1=6 THEN P3=5
5290 DU(P2,P3)=SP:GOTO5040
5300 IF AD$[X]<>"I"THEN5040
5310 PRINT"I'VE BEEN KILLED.":INPUT"NEW
GAME";EI$:IFLEFT$(EI$,1)="Y"THENRUN
5311 PRINT" ":END
5500 R1$=AD$[X+1]+AD$[X+2]:X=X+1:PA=VAL(
R1$):RETURN
5600 R1$=AD$[X+1]:X=X+1:PA=VAL(R1$):RETU
RN
5700 P1=VAL(AD$[X+1]):P2=VAL(AD$[X+2]):X
=X+2:RETURN
6000 PRINT"YOU'VE WON THE GAME.":INPUT"N
EW GAME";EI$:IFLEFT$(EI$,1)="Y"THENRUN

READY.
```

Appendix A

Special Printer Listing Codes

All the programs in this book were listed using the TURBOPRINT / GT printer interface in the special listing mode. This should make the Commodore graphic symbols easier to enter and with less error. Compare the TURPOPRINT listing on page 88 with the standard Commodore listing on page 98, the screen of GOLD FEVER.

Below are the special listing codes produced in the special listing mode and the equalivent Commodore keys.

TURBOPRINT/GT	Commodore key
(WHT)	CTRL 2 [WHITE]
(RVS)	CTRL 9 REVERSE ON
(HOM)	CLR/HOME
(RED)	CTRL 3 [RED]
(RHT)	RIGHT CURSOR
(GRN)	CTRL 6 [GREEN]
(BLU)	CTRL 7 [BLUE]
(SH*)	SHIFT *
(SHA)	SHIFT A
(SHB)	SHIFT B
(SHC)	SHIFT C
(SHD)	SHIFT D
(SHE)	SHIFT E
(SHF)	SHIFT F
(SHG)	SHIFT G
(SHH)	SHIFT H
(SHI)	SHIFT I
(SHJ)	SHIFT J

(SHK)	SHIFT K
(SHL)	SHIFT L
(SHM)	SHIFT M
(SHN)	SHIFT M
(SHO)	SHIFT O
(SHP)	SHIFT P
(SHQ)	SHIFT Q
(SHR)	SHIFT R
(SHS)	SHIFT S
(SHT)	SHIFT T
(SHU)	SHIFT U
(SHV)	SHIFT V
(SHW)	SHIFT W
(SHX)	SHIFT X
(SHY)	SHIFT Y
(SHZ)	SHIFT Z
(SH+)	SHIFT +
[CM-]	CMDR -
(SH-)	SHIFT -
(PI)	SHIFT ↑
(CM*)	CMDR *
(CM1)	CMDR 1 [ORANGE]
(BLK)	CTRL 1 [BLACK]
(UP)	SHIFT UP/CURSOR
(OFF)	CTRL O REVERSE OFF
(CLR)	SHIFT CLR/HOME
(CM2)	CMDR 2 [BROWN]
(CM3)	CMDR 3 [L RED]
(CM4)	CMDR 4 [GRAY 1]
(CM6)	CMDR 6 [L GREEN]
(CM7)	CMDR 7 [L BLUE]
(LFT)	SHIFT LEFT/CURSOR
(YEL)	CTRL 8 [YELLOW]

{CYN}	CTRL 4 [CYAN]
{SH }	SHIFT SPACE
{CMK}	CMDR K
{CMI}	CMDR I
{CMT}	CMDR T
{CM@}	CMDR @
{CMG}	CMDR G
{CM+}	CMDR +
{CMM}	CMDR M
{SH#}	SHIFT POUND SIGN
{CMN}	CMDR N
{CMQ}	CMDR Q
{CMD}	CMDR D
{CMZ}	CMDR Z
{CMS}	CMDR S
{CMP}	CMDR P
{CMA}	CMDR A
{CME}	CMDR E
{CMR}	CMDR R
{CMW}	CMDR W
{CMH}	CMDR H
{CMJ}	CMDR J
{CML}	CMDR L
{CMY}	CMDR Y
{CMU}	CMDR U
{CMO}	CMDR O
{SH@}	SHIFT @
{CMF}	CMDR F
{CMC}	CMDR C
{CMX}	CMDR X
{CMV}	CMDR V
{CMB}	CMDR B

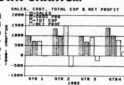

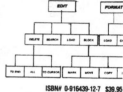

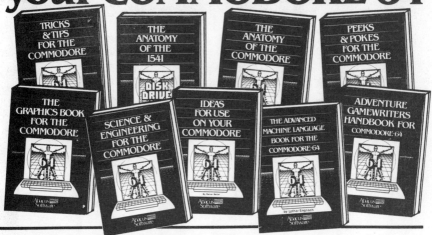